GWEN FORD FAULKENBERRY

JESUS
Be Near Me

60 DEVOTIONS
FOR A CLOSER WALK WITH GOD

summerside
PRESS

Summerside Press™
Minneapolis 55337
www.summersidepress.com

Jesus, Be Near Me

© 2011 by Gwen Ford Faulkenberry

ISBN 978-1-60936-231-7

Scripture references are from the following sources: The Holy Bible, King James
Version (KJV). The Holy Bible, New International Version®, NIV®. Copyright © 1973,
1978, 1984, 2011 by Biblica, Inc.™ Used by permission of Zondervan. All rights
reserved worldwide. The New King James Version (NKJV). Copyright © 1982 by
Thomas Nelson, Inc. Used by permission. The New American Standard Bible®
(NASB), Copyright © 1960, 1962, 1963, 1968, 1971, 1972, 1973, 1975, 1977, 1995 by The
Lockman Foundation. Used by permission. The Holy Bible, New Living Translation
(NLT), copyright 1996, 2004, 2007. Used by permission of Tyndale House Publishers,
Inc., Wheaton, Illinois. The New Century Version® (NCV). Copyright © 1987, 1988,
1991, 2005 by Thomas Nelson, Inc. Used by permission.

Stock or custom editions of Summerside Press titles may be purchased in bulk for
educational, business, ministry, fundraising, or sales promotional use.
For information, please e-mail specialmarkets@summersidepress.com.

Cover and interior design by Lookout Design, Inc. | www.lookoutdesign.com
Cover Photo: © Jill Battaglia/Arcangel Images

*Summerside Press is an inspirational publisher offering fresh,
irresistible books to uplift the heart and engage the mind.*

Printed in China.

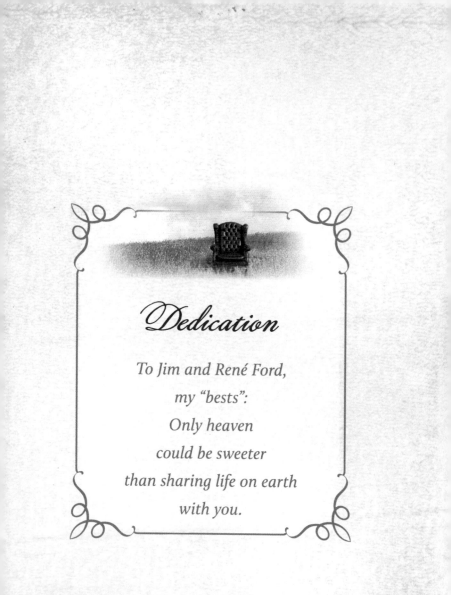

Dedication

To Jim and René Ford,
my "bests":
Only heaven
could be sweeter
than sharing life on earth
with you.

Contents

Preface

I've written a couple of other devotional books, and to be honest, those came pretty easily. The words seemed to spill out of my heart and onto the page as fast as I could type. It was lovely. At the time I chalked it up to a move of God. There's nothing like it when the Spirit is flowing through your life, causing things to come together; it's just amazing. You just stand back in awe and wonder at His handiwork. It's a Christian writer's dream and miraculous to watch.

Those books were about God's beauty and the beauty He creates out of our lives. When I sent the proposal to my publisher for a third book of devotions, I thought I'd stay with a broad theme like beauty. It was working for me. I liked the title *Deeper*, and proposed to write a book about the deeper life we can experience in Christ. The publisher came back and said, in a nutshell, "We like you, and we like your idea about the inner life. But we want a devotional book that focuses on Jesus."

That didn't sound too hard at the time. After all, I love Jesus. I've always agreed with the DaySpring card that reads, "When you get down to it, all that really matters is Jesus."

So why did I spend several weeks in a cold sweat, staring at a blank computer screen till my eyeballs felt like they were going to fall out of my head?

I believe it has something to do with the fact that, as C.S. Lewis writes in *The Lion, The Witch and The Wardrobe*, "Who said anything about safe? 'Course [Jesus] isn't safe. But he's good."

The good part is easy. It's the unsafe nature of Jesus that can be a problem, at least for me. As I poured over other people's writings on the subject, I kept noticing a pattern. There are a few really good books. Then there are many that teach *about* Jesus, like a biology textbook in the sense that He is a fish to be dissected. In these, He becomes so distinctly *other*— existentially—so that the relationship we have is no longer personal.

The pendulum also swings in the opposite direction. I read other books, some devotions, that were so personal I was put off by them. I can't know another's heart or experience, but I know that Jesus is *not* my homeboy. He's not something I can contain. In other words, He's a good lion, but He's still a lion. And that fact demands that I approach Him with reverence and awe.

To be successful, this book needed to transcend these two poles, but I felt stymied in the middle. So the computer screen stayed empty. I wrote, deleted, and prayed. Finally an e-mail came from a dear friend at Summerside:

Read Ephesians 3:14–20 today, about the fullness of God in us. Paul prayed this for the Ephesians, and I am praying it for you. Dwell on it. Just sit there a bit and ponder the amazing fact that His love is working in our lives, making our Spirits strong. Paul says God's power, working within us, can do far more than anything we could imagine. God's power. Not ours....I'm hoping you will rest on that and not delete too much and leave some room for the "far more than anything you could imagine."

That was the word my heart needed. Like Lewis' Lucy Pevensie, I climbed on the back of the Lion and let Him take me wherever He wanted me to go. These little devotions are notes I took along the journey.

Jesus, Lion of Judah and King of my existence, here is my offering. I pour it out at Your feet. I pray Your Spirit will breathe life into the words I've written, blowing away all but the ones that will be a blessing to Your heart, and the hearts of those who turn these pages, looking for glimpses of You.

Author's Introduction

*I*f you're one of those people who have it all together, this book is probably not for you. You might want to look for something by a writer who's an expert. Somebody a lot more qualified than me.

You see, I'm really a nobody on the subject of getting near Jesus. I'm just a fellow traveler. One of the crowd standing on her tippy-toes to get a glimpse of Him; or more likely, the outcast chasing Him down, clutching after His garment. Like her, I don't have the inside scoop. I just know I want to be whole.

Martin Luther once said, "We preach best what we need to learn most." That's becoming my motto for devotional writing. I'd be lying if I said, *"Jesus, Be Near Me* is a how-to manual for being close to Jesus; just follow these sixty easy steps and you're there." Nope.

I don't believe there's a specific procedure to follow. If one exists, I've never found it, and I've done a fair amount of searching. Instead, this book is the cry of my heart. Plain and simple: I need Jesus to be near me. I don't want to live a day without His presence.

Come to think of it, maybe that's why writing these devotions became so cathartic for me. Because I—myself—so desperately needed to learn what it means to have Him near.

Gwen Ford Faulkenberry
Ozark, Arkansas
February 2011

Near and Dear

I say these things...so that they may have
the full measure of my joy within them.

JOHN 17:13 NIV

*T*hese words from John 17 come from the prayer that Jesus prayed at the time of His crucifixion—for His disciples and for us (the disciples to come). They express a desire that He had for all of His followers to experience His fullness. *A full measure of my joy.*

The prayer, *Jesus, Be Near Me*, expresses the desire of our hearts when we long to be closer to Him. Sometimes it may be a simple request. Other times, probably more often, for most of us it is a cry from deep within our souls—*Be near me in my distress! Be near me in my hurts! Be near me in my doubts and fears! Be near me through the storm!*

I believe during these times it is important to remember Jesus' prayer for us. It is easy to understand, in our human condition, why we would need Jesus and feel the desire to have Him near. As my Dad says, we are a needy people. We need help, wisdom, blessing, strength, comfort, grace, love, hope, joy—all of the things Jesus is. Our deep desire for Him is eclipsed by only one thing: His longing to be near to us. He is longing to be near me. *Me.*

Tears roll down my cheeks as I write this. What a mind-boggling truth it is that Jesus wants us near—wanted us even when we didn't want Him. He wanted us badly enough to die so that He could bring us near! Even after all of these years of being a Christian and experiencing the wonders of His presence, I still find myself cringing—hoping, doubting that He would really want to be near me. It's hard to comprehend such a radical love.

After all, why would He want to be near *me*? I'm not always easy to be around. I'm not exactly what you'd call low-maintenance; I'd try the patience of any lesser God. Furthermore, I'm not much to look at. Not the sharpest crayon in the box. I lose my temper, make stupid decisions, and am not always a lot of fun. It's like Einstein hanging out with a physics class dropout or Mr. Universe dating a mousy, bookish nerd. Why would He do that? Maybe you can relate?

And yet, when He was on the way to the cross, we were on His mind. He prayed for me—and you—to have His fullness.

Not just a little bit of Him. All of the fullness of His joy. We don't have to cringe or coax Him to be near us. He died so that's where He could always stay—near me.

How thankful I am, my dear, beloved Jesus, that You actually want to be near me. I pray that I won't ever let anything get in Your way. Know that in my heart and life You have the open invitation: Be near me today, tomorrow, and forever. I want to walk in the fullness of Your joy.

Believing Is Seeing

Come and see.

JOHN 1:39 KJV

*I*n my Bible, the context of the above verse is labeled "The First Disciples." It's a scene that has fascinated me since the first time I read John 1.

Imagine this: John the Baptist is standing there with two of his followers and spots Jesus walking by. John calls out, "Behold, the Lamb of God!" And apparently, instead of stopping to chat with His cousin, Jesus keeps on walking. The two guys with John decide to follow Jesus. Verse 38 says (rather ironically it seems), that *when Jesus turned and saw them following Him*, He asks them a question. As if He didn't know they were going to follow. As if He didn't know the answer to the question before He asked it.

"What are you looking for?"

I wonder what they felt in the moment He asked that. Did His eyes pierce theirs with an all-seeing gaze? Did His words pass through the men's ears and down into their hearts? Were they stirred in their spirits—moved somewhere deep in their souls? Their answer, like His question, seems to suggest a meaning deeper than just what's on the surface:

"Master, where do You dwell?"

Jesus' answer is simple: "Come and see."

It is with these words that scholars mark the calling of the first followers of Jesus. They came, they saw where He lived, and the world was never the same. A few verses later Nathanael questions Philip about Jesus and Philip echoes the invitation. Indeed, the call comes down through the ages to extend to us today: "Come and see."

Sometimes I wish I could have been there in person when Jesus said that. Wouldn't believing have been so much easier then? If I could have walked with Him and talked with Him... to have seen where He lived and seen Him in action for myself. Changing water into wine. Turning over tables in the temple. Calming the sea. After all, seeing is believing, right?

Or is it? There's a praise song we used to sing at our church that says, "Open the eyes of my heart, Lord, I want to see You." I like to sing it because it expresses my deepest longing, to truly see Him and know Him. To see His glory. His power. His grace.

Like the disciples, I need to see Him myself before I can begin to share Him with others. I'd like to get so close I could describe the lines on His face. But, how do we *see* Someone who is invisible?

Maybe it's not ironic that the Bible says Jesus noticed the disciples were following Him. Maybe there's a principle there. It was *after* those first guys chose to follow Jesus that they were invited to see where He lived. Such a detail is probably in there for people like me, who need to remember that with Jesus, believing comes *before* seeing. Even with the disciples, who had Him there in the flesh, the heart was the first thing Jesus was concerned with—not the eyes.

What are you looking for today? What am I? Sometimes it's way too easy for my eyes—and heart—to wander away from the One who is the Way to life. I am trying to take one step toward Him, believing. According to John 1, that's the way we'll get to see where He dwells.

Jesus, I want to see You. Draw me nearer; take me deeper. I want to see— and stay—where You dwell.

Jesus Street

*If anyone loves Me, he will keep My word; and My Father will love him,
and We will come to him and make Our home with him.*

JOHN 14:23 NKJV

Stone and I are friends with a couple named Roy and
Char who live about two hours away from our home
in an area where we lived when we were fresh out of college. We
were part of a couples Bible study which met at their house. Filling their living room on Wednesday nights, we affectionately
dubbed our meetings "Couch Church."

Couch Church was a great time. There were always mugs
of hot tea and coffee. Char usually made some yummy dessert
like oatmeal cookies that were passed around on a chintz plate.
Roy taught the Bible from his heart, a deep reservoir of spiritual
experience. As it was early in our marriage, we learned some
things that are still foundational to who we are as a family today.

Because Roy and Char are so special to us, we like to go back and visit them as often as possible. They are like spiritual parents to us, and after all we've experienced through their hospitality, their house feels a little bit like a second home to us.

Imagine my shock when I called Char to plan a visit and she told me she and Roy were moving! They had just sold the house where they lived for over thirty years and at that moment were in the process of moving into a new one in the same town. Since the new house was all one level with a smaller yard they felt it to be perfect for this stage of their lives.

I could hear the excitement in Char's voice. I shared it because I was happy for her but felt a little sad because I'd become attached to their old home. It held so many memories Stone and I cherish. I asked her how she felt about leaving the home where she raised her children.

"At first I thought it might feel strange," Char told me. "But, then I realized that nothing important has changed. We may live on a different street, but our address is the Lord's presence. Jesus is with us—His presence is where we live."

When Stone and I went to visit their new home, we found what Char said to be absolutely true. The walls were a different color and the rooms in different positions, but their new house was full of Jesus. We could see His light in their eyes as they greeted us at the front door. Feel His touch in their warm hugs. His encouragement echoed in their words, and the air seemed scented with the sweet fragrance of His love. Even the couches—in their new environment—still exuded the comfort of His fellowship!

Home and everything it means—security, safety, comfort, and joy, to name a few things—can't be found within four walls. How old or new, even the street address is totally irrelevant. Home is found in Jesus! And He's with us wherever we go. His presence truly is our home.

> *Thank You, Jesus, that no matter*
>
> *where I go, You are with me.*
>
> *My address is Your Presence.*
>
> *It is with You, in You,*
>
> *and for You that I live.*

He Who Sees

Earth's crammed with heaven,
And every common bush afire with God,
But only he who sees takes off his shoes.

ELIZABETH BARRETT BROWNING

I was blessed as a child to have many people in my life who loved God and did their best to nurture my faith in Jesus. One person who made an indelible impact on my life was Larry Johnston, the father of one of my best friends. He was not the most educated, nor the richest person in our community, and he certainly wasn't perfect, but he had something most others didn't: a heart that sees.

Larry was a big, strong man with shoulders that seemed broad enough to hold up the world. He had huge, ruggedly beautiful hands that were rough from hard work, and he had a laugh as loud as thunder. He was my Sunday school teacher. Every week I looked forward to—and dreaded—his hugs. My backbones crackled when he picked me up off the ground. The question he asked me every week at the door was, "How did you get so beautiful?" And, I was supposed to answer, "God made me this way." It was like a quiz. He never let me pass without the right answer.

As I grew, Larry's presence in my life was a constant reminder of the Lord's loving care. Sometimes, when I was in college, I would answer the phone on the day of a test and it would be him, quoting a verse from the Bible and offering to pray with me. He never knew when my tests were; the Spirit simply prompted him to call.

After I married, my husband grew to love Larry too. He likes to tell the story about when he and my brother were eating in a restaurant and Larry walked in and joined them. The conversation soon turned to Jesus—Larry's favorite subject—and as he paraphrased these verses from Joshua, he began to get really worked up:

> Now when Joshua was near Jericho, he looked up and saw a man standing in front of him with a drawn sword in His hand. Joshua went up to Him and asked, "Are you for us or for our enemies?"
>
> "Neither," He replied, "But as commander of the army of the LORD I have now come" (Joshua 5:13–14 NIV).

At this point my husband said Larry's face was streaming with tears. "Boys," he said, as he rapped the backs of their necks, "Jesus didn't come to take sides. He came to take charge!" That dining experience was anything but ordinary.

Years later, we rushed to the hospital where Larry was recovering from emergency surgery. As my husband prayed over him, we reminded our friend of that story and that Jesus was still in charge. He clasped our hands and cried. In the following months, as he battled cancer, Larry continued to point me to Jesus. I think of him when I read about the one "who sees" in the quote by Elizabeth Barrett Browning, and I hope to follow his example.

Jesus, I want to be one who sees
You here on earth. Like Larry,
let me be a person who stands humbly
on holy ground, and testifies
to Your glory till my very last breath.

Jesus Happens

In him was life, and that life was the light of all mankind.

JOHN 1:4 NIV

I'm on the edge this morning. I'm sitting at my desk in a lovely office with flowers, pictures of my precious family, and a wonderful wing-backed chair. It's quiet. A perfect place to work. This is a place where I usually feel comfortable, safe, and happy. And yet I'm not comfortable. I'm in no physical danger that I know of, but I do not feel safe. And I'm definitely not happy.

While I sit here, breathing the scent of fresh hyacinths a student brought me, someone I love is miles away in a doctor's sterile-smelling office. Right about now a long needle is poking through her skin and making its way to her liver to extract a sample of cells from a spot detected earlier on a CT scan. She is scared. I'm scared too. We won't know anything today.

Even when we know the results of the biopsy, we won't know everything, and I hate not knowing. I'm studying the walls of my office thinking about going for a climb.

And yet, I am reminded. *We do know one thing.*

Paul writes, "For I am convinced that neither death nor life, neither angels nor demons, neither the present nor the future, nor any powers, neither height nor depth, nor anything else in all creation, will be able to separate us from the love of God that is in Christ Jesus our Lord" (Romans 8:38–39 NIV).

We know that Jesus loves us. This truth is so easy to accept when things are going well. For me the love of Jesus seemed tangible on the days my children were born. They were (and are) undisputed miracles I can touch with my hands. Lesser miracles like a hug from my husband or even seeing from my deck the sight of a lavender sunset over the river fill my heart with a sense of His nearness. Those are times I feel so blessed. So loved.

But today feelings of love are overshadowed by a sense of gathering doom. I cannot take false security in things that go well, because things are not going well today. And whether the biopsy turns out good or bad this time, one day my loved one and I both—and every other person—will face something we can't lick. Life happens. Our health, wealth, and happiness can, and do, turn on a dime.

My friend Roy Lessin writes in his book *Jesus, Name Above*

All Names, that when people say, "life happens," they really mean that "circumstances happen." He adds, "Jesus is the life that happens in us, and the life of Jesus can be our reality no matter what the circumstances." Isn't that the truth?

In my office today I have a choice. It's the same choice my loved one at the doctor's office—and all of us—must make. We can choose to succumb to the terror of the unknown, or we can choose to take comfort in the love of Jesus. Instead of climbing the walls, we can run like little children into His arms and find refuge there in the midst of any circumstances.

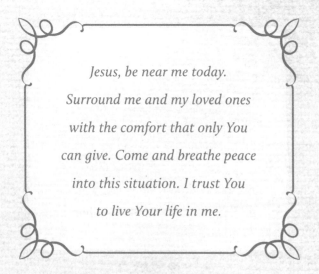

Jesus, be near me today.
Surround me and my loved ones
with the comfort that only You
can give. Come and breathe peace
into this situation. I trust You
to live Your life in me.

Mr. Right

As the bridegroom rejoices over the bride,

so your God will rejoice over you.

ISAIAH 62:5 NASB

Being a hopeless romantic, I've always loved weddings. As a little girl I drew out plans for my own future wedding day. I created a variety of dresses in my head, and imagined extravagant floral designs that would cover the sanctuary of my church. Even now I get excited when I receive an invitation to a wedding. I'm always curious to see how the venue will be decorated, what music will be chosen, and what the people involved will wear. I like to study the interesting dynamics between people too. It's such an emotional day for the bride and groom and all of their loved ones, a day when one chapter of life ends and a new one begins.

One of the best days of my life was my own wedding day, when I got to dress up like a fairytale princess and marry the handsome prince. It was seven o'clock in the evening on New Year's Eve. My dad cradled my arm in his big hand like a piece of fine china. As the bridal march sounded, we walked down the aisle, past smiling faces of well-wishers. My heart felt like it might beat out of my chest. Then I saw him: my prince—Stone Faulkenberry—the one my heart loves.

He stood at the end of the aisle in a black tux with tails, tall and strong and beautiful. I saw his profile first through the crowd, the Roman nose, square jaw, and broad shoulders. As I moved closer, his face was revealed—resplendent with joy. His shining blue eyes were fixed on me and me alone. My racing heart stilled. In that moment I felt completely loved, completely honored, completely home. Moving forward to take his hand, nothing else mattered except that I was his and he was mine.

Sometimes it's hard for me to imagine the God of the universe taking this kind of delight in human beings, but He does. Jesus calls Himself our bridegroom in Matthew 25. It's the perfect analogy for perfect love. Picture this: The Prince stands on the threshold of heaven in all of His amazing glory. Majesty and light surround Him. A golden crown blazes on His head. With shining eyes He looks down through time and finds me, even in my less-than-a-princess state—and He finds you. A radiant smile breaks out across His face. His fiery eyes glow with pride. From that moment forward, nothing else matters, because we are His, and He is ours.

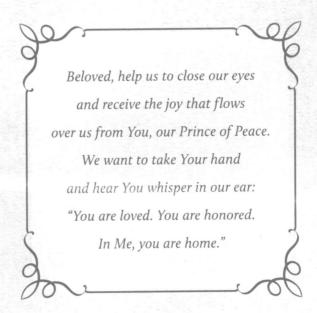

Beloved, help us to close our eyes
and receive the joy that flows
over us from You, our Prince of Peace.
We want to take Your hand
and hear You whisper in our ear:
"You are loved. You are honored.
In Me, you are home."

Toasted

Then Jesus declared, "I am the bread of Life. Whoever comes to me will never go hungry, and whoever believes in me will never be thirsty."

John 6:35 niv

One of our family pastimes when we're driving a long distance is to look for wayside pulpits (those message boards outside of churches). Sometimes we come across a good one that seems tailored to a particular moment. A few years ago, on the way to Florida, we were in the middle of a deep theological discussion about monsters under the bed. Harper, especially, was having a hard time with the idea of sleeping alone (a new experience for him at age six). Nothing seemed to be helping until one of the kids spotted a marquee that read, "Fear not, for I am with you." We all agreed that this was quite literally a sign from God.

Other times we are not so fortunate in our findings.

Besides containing appalling grammatical errors, it seems at times church signs can be abrasive, communicating ideas that seem counter-productive to their author's intended meaning. For example, last week my kids and I passed a church with a billboard that read: "Without the bread of life you are toast."

Reflective of her name, my ten-year-old daughter Grace commented, "Well, *that's* not very encouraging."

Adelaide, three, cracked up.

Harper, who at eight shows a propensity for becoming a modern-day prophet, observed, "It may not be tactful, but it's the truth."

I tried to withhold my judgment. I want my kids to think for themselves, reason things out, and come to their own conclusions. It's funny, though. They always seem to want my opinion most of all when I'm trying not to give it. When they pressed me on the issue of the sign, I said, "Well, actually, I can't stand signs that say stuff like that. If I wasn't a Christian, a threat on a sign certainly wouldn't make me want to be one."

They gaped at me, wide-eyed. I think they were shocked by my passion.

Instantly, I felt a pang of conviction. It was followed by a still, small voice. *Those are pretty strong words. You* can't stand *signs like that? Really?* He persisted: *Did you ever suppose that there are all kinds of people in the Kingdom of God? Every church* sign you read, just like every sermon you hear, doesn't have to be your cup of tea. Do you want your kids to be critical thinkers, or do you want them harboring a critical spirit?

I'll admit I struggle with that. There seems to be a fine line between those two things, and I'm good at stepping over it. After confessing my weakness to God I also discussed it with my kids that night, and tried to explain the difference between thinking critically and being too critical. The inevitable question became, "How do we know which is which?"

That's the big question, isn't it? I obviously don't always know. When it comes down to it, there's not a perfect formula. Just like everything else in the Christian life, we have to rely on Jesus to show us the way, moment by moment.

The next time I passed that sign on my way to work, the irony of it hit me like a flying toaster. Without His presence to guide me, as a parent or otherwise, I really *am* toast.

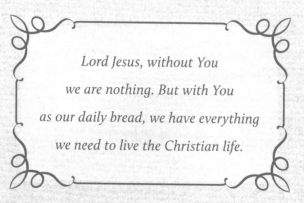

Lord Jesus, without You
we are nothing. But with You
as our daily bread, we have everything
we need to live the Christian life.

This Little Light of Mine

I am the light of the world. Whoever follows me will never walk in darkness, but will have the light of life.

JOHN 8:12 NIV

Not long ago I was sitting at a ballgame in my usual spot at half-court. I was watching my second-grade son warm up along with all of his teammates and also keeping an eye on his handsome coach who just happens to be my husband. Grace, Adelaide, and several members of my family were there.

A few moments into the first quarter, a woman I barely knew sat down beside me. I smiled at her and said hello, just being polite. No harm in being friendly. Sometimes that can be a mistake, however. People can get the wrong idea and think you're actually interested in them. Like this lady. She seemed to want to talk, but I tried to make it obvious that I didn't. I wasn't there to make friends. I was there to watch my son play basketball.

This particular woman has a reputation for being... peculiar. I believe the word I heard someone use to describe her was "certifiable." Between cheers for her kid, she went on and on in my ear about how she played basketball as a teenager, what her husband was like, etc. Nodding occasionally, I mostly tuned her out. After all, doesn't a godly mother put the support of her children above other distractions? There was a peewee game in progress, and my son had just scored a basket. He required my full attention.

The woman finally got the message around halftime. She turned to someone else—anyone else—who would listen and act like they cared about what she had to say. I pushed her further to the periphery of my mind as our team went on to win the game.

The next day at church a friend spoke about Jesus being the light of the world, and how when He comes into our lives He doesn't provide just enough light for us. Instead, He gives us all He has, and that's enough light to share with everyone. We read the Scripture, "Do not forget to do good and share with others, for with such sacrifices God is pleased" (Hebrews 13:16 NIV). I thought about that lady at the ballgame and how needy she was. And I thought about how I just turned away from her, absorbed as I was with my own life and kids. I didn't even stop to consider what Jesus would do with her.

He'd have found a way to manage both, even if it meant inviting her and her child for ice cream—or perhaps a little tea and sympathy—after the game.

Sometimes we hide our lights because we are afraid to let them shine. Sometimes we are too busy shining our lights on someone else. But Jesus has reminded me that those in darkness sometimes come and sit right next to us. All we have to do is open up our hearts and share His light.

Jesus, give me Your compassion
for those who live in darkness.
Help me not to turn away just because
it's not convenient, or because I feel
uncomfortable. Most of all take away
my selfishness. Let Your light shine so
brightly in me that others may see You.

God With Us

So do not fear, for I am with you; do not be dismayed,
for I am your God. I will strengthen you and help you.

ISAIAH 41:10 NIV

A few years ago my sister-in-law had a miscarriage. Afterward, she suffered from severe depression and anxiety attacks and had to take medication to recover. It took her and my brother a year to gather their courage to try again for another baby.

On Christmas Eve, they handed out Christmas cards to all of the family. These cards were signed, "Jim, René, Madeline, Sophia, and Baby Ford." I think my mother and I simultaneously squealed for joy as the surprise reached our eyes and trickled into our hearts. Tears ran down our cheeks, and prayers of thanksgiving filled our home as we all joined in a group hug.

The next few days were pure celebration. We always enjoy our family traditions of baking, caroling, and gathering together, but this time was particularly sweet. René opened a "Baby's First Christmas" outfit—for the next year—and we all dreamed together about whether the baby would be a boy or girl and brainstormed ideas for names.

They had scheduled the first doctor's appointment during Christmas break. None of us imagined that, as before, there would be no heartbeat. René and Jim were encouraged that it was still very early, perhaps too early, to detect. A hormone test was ordered.

When the doctor called with the test results, we were with Rene. I will never forget her face, how it crumpled in pain, and the sobs that followed as the doctor delivered the news that the baby in her womb was dead. We wrapped ourselves around her like a cocoon and all cried together. Personally, I felt like a sword pierced through my very soul.

René is like a sister to me, and as much as I could enter into her pain, I did. But, we human beings are limited in our ability to soothe and heal. I could not be with her every moment. I could not put comfort inside her head. Even my brother Jim, who stood beside her and suffered with her, could not heal her heart. Only Jesus has the power to do that.

At one of the lowest points in the aftermath, René told me

she woke up in a cold sweat in the middle of the night. It was pitch black, and Jim was beside her, asleep. She felt the darkness of her loss begin to creep over her. She was completely desperate. Feeling suffocated, she said all she could do was cry out to Jesus for mercy.

It was then that a miracle occurred. Jesus answered. René says He spoke three words to her heart: *I am here.* Peace breathed over her spirit like a fresh wind.

When we are in the darkest places, when others cannot reach us, God can. When we cry out to Him, He cries with us, surrounds us, loves us. We don't have to understand that, but we sure can build our faith on it.

*Thank You, Jesus, that You
never leave me nor forsake me.
I know Your grace is sufficient
for my every need, and I receive it today.
I trust that You are enough for me.*

Lolita in Tehran

The LORD does not look at the things man looks at. Man looks at the
outward appearance, but the LORD looks at the heart.

1 SAMUEL 16:7 NIV

In a book that makes me glad I'm an English instructor in America rather than Iran, Azar Nafisi writes about her experiences teaching literature to Iranian college students. She taught at the University of Tehran, and as the regime in power grew stricter and stricter, virtually every book she thought was important to teach was banned. Instead of cowing to this attempt at government control over education, Nafisi decided to hold class in her home. A banned book club, if you will. There were many times as I was reading the tale that I had to remind myself these were not rebel Christians hiding in order to worship Jesus. These were just kids, mostly young women, who just wanted to read Jane Austen and *The Great Gatsby*.

A particularly powerful image I remember from this book, *Reading Lolita in Tehran*, is when a group of female students come through Nafisi's door. Disguised in burqas that covered everything but their eyes, they began to shed their outer garments as soon as they were safe inside her foyer. It is then that each one came to life, according to the writer. Their individual characters emerged like butterflies from cocoons.

This story brings to light many issues which are essential to Christian women. Perhaps the most readily recognizable is the image of the outer coverings, something to which I believe all women who read this book can probably relate. The covering doesn't have to be a burqa. It may be the clothing one's Christian denomination approves. Or the creed. It may be the wearing of makeup. The fixing of hair. Or the not. It may be a talent or degree, or the lack of either one. What about skin color? Bank account? Disability? Dress size? Ouch. It may even be a smile that says, "everything's okay" or a frown that says, "don't come too close."

With us, just like the women in Professor Nafisi's book, it is when we peel off those outer layers, letting other people see what's underneath, that we truly can be free. Hidden behind our veils of pride, shame, pretension, fear—insert here whatever your particular veils may be—we isolate ourselves from others. It's a form of bondage, and Jesus came to set the captive free!

As with the literary ladies, freedom happens only in places where we feel safe and secure. When one person takes the risk of being known, letting another see below the surface, that gives the other person the courage to remove her layers. Often it's painful. Sometimes we find layers we didn't even know existed, in ourselves and others. Almost always the process involves risk. But freedom to be who we are in Christ—and giving other people that same freedom—is worth it. As Paul writes, "It was for freedom that Christ set us free."

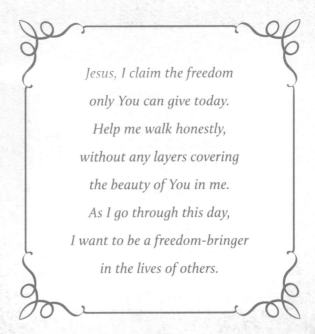

Jesus, I claim the freedom
only You can give today.
Help me walk honestly,
without any layers covering
the beauty of You in me.
As I go through this day,
I want to be a freedom-bringer
in the lives of others.

What a Wonderful World

And God saw everything that he had made,
and, behold, it was very good.

Genesis 1:31 kjv

One of my favorite things I have read is an essay written by Christian Wiman called "Gazing into the Abyss." I ran across it after reading his book of poetry, *Every Riven Thing*, and became obsessed enough to research the author. There are many things in the essay—and in Wiman's poetry—that I find to be faith-affirming. One particular quote struck a chord with me:

> *I was brought up with the poisonous notion that you had to renounce love of the earth in order to receive the love of God. My experience has been just the opposite: a love of the earth and existence so overflowing that it implied, or included, or even absolutely demanded, God.*

I suppose I love this idea so much because my experience has been similar to Wiman's in regard to sensing and celebrating God's presence in the world. In John 17, Jesus prays, "not that You take them out of the world but that You protect them from the evil one" (v. 15 NIV). In verse eighteen He goes on to say, "As You sent Me into the world, I have sent them into the world." Of course I believe He sends us to the world to be His witnesses, but I also believe we're in the world to witness Him, in all of His creative glory, in every flower petal and cricket's song.

I read an article in *The New Yorker* magazine a while back that contained a denouncement of "New Atheism" for the very same reason. Terry Eagleton, a literary critic from Oxford, argued that atheistic thinking strips humanity of language that expresses the miraculous in our everyday lives. Who can hear a Beethoven symphony without recognizing that there is something—Someone—who transcends us, and yet connects with us? Is His signature not written on every sunset? Can we not see glimpses of His beauty in the eyes of a little child?

I believe, if our desire is to draw near to Jesus, we can find Him every day in the world. He has not abandoned us to some awful place. On the contrary, He is here, working among us. Think about it. Why would the One who "so loved the world" that He gave Himself for it (John 3:16), demand that we renounce it in order to receive Him? This earth is a hard place.

But it's also beautiful. We are showered with His blessings through the love of family and friends. We are gifted with joy and purpose. His splendor is manifested all around—in creation, and in the lives of His created ones.

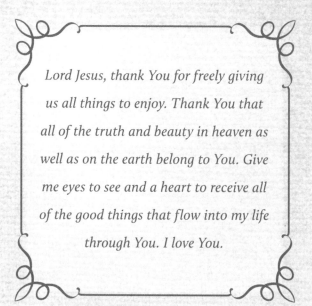

Lord Jesus, thank You for freely giving us all things to enjoy. Thank You that all of the truth and beauty in heaven as well as on the earth belong to You. Give me eyes to see and a heart to receive all of the good things that flow into my life through You. I love You.

Bart, the Female Cat

He chose us in Him before the foundation of the world,

that we should be holy and without blame before Him in love,

having predestined us to adoption as sons by Jesus Christ to Himself,

according to the good pleasure of His will, to the praise of the glory

of His grace, by which He made us accepted in the Beloved.

EPHESIANS 1:4–6 NKJV

We have five cats. One of them is named Bart, though she is a female cat. Harper picked her out because he was convinced no one else at the shelter would want her. She came with her name, and though we have tried other, more feminine ones, we have not been able to change it. Bart kind of stuck.

Bart is the friendliest of all of our cats. She waits by the back door looking for any opportunity to run inside the house. She loves to lounge on the couch or one of our beds, and is happiest when we're petting or playing with her. However, she usually bites us when we try to remove her from the house. Bart is thoroughly convinced she should be an inside cat.

The other day I tried to pick up Bart from where she was sprawled out in the sun on my daughters' bed. As usual, she scratched at me, and I had to hold her in that certain place on the back of her neck in order to carry her outside so she wouldn't bite my hand. Setting her down outside the door so she could use the facilities, I laughed. "Poor Bart. You are so misunderstood."

Although Bart seems to have a clear sense of who she is and where she belongs, regardless of her name, if she was a person she might have an identity crisis. As Christians we can also have identity issues. Our true identities get buried under labels others give us, or even titles we give ourselves: daughter, wife, sister, mother, teacher, doctor, cashier. What about Baptist, Methodist, Presbyterian, and Catholic? Ever been called a loser? What about a freak?

Though the last two are unhealthy, there's nothing wrong with wearing different hats at certain times. Most of us do play a lot of roles. But regardless of the circumstance, it's important to keep our center—to know who we are at the core.

Bart knows she is a princess. It doesn't matter what she's called, and that's like us too. We are children of the King. His presence in our lives defines our identity. Who we really are is who

He says we are. His bride. His precious child. His masterpiece.

There is such joy and security in defining ourselves by God's terms rather than those assigned to us by others, or even ourselves. Roles assigned to us by people usually come with strings attached to our performance. If we perform well, we may make a good name for ourselves. However, that good name can be changed or lost in the event of our failure to perform. The identity forged for us at the cross is different. That's because it's not based on our performance, but His.

Jesus, the perfect One, is our center. Because of Him, we are beloved right where we are. He chose us, adopted us, and gave us the only identity that counts. We are His.

Jesus, thank You that my true identity is found in You, and Your opinion of me never changes. You love me. I am valuable to You. May Your love, at the core of my being, extend outward in all of the roles I play in life. I want You and You alone to define who I really am.

Help My Unbelief

These things have I written unto you that believe on the name of the Son of God; that ye may know that ye have eternal life.

1 JOHN 5:13 KJV

Last week Stone and I were in bed, almost asleep, when we heard the pitter-patter of little feet. Ten-year-old feet, to be exact. It was Grace. We switched on the light, and she came and sat on our bed, eyes brimming with tears.

"Mommy and Daddy, do you ever have doubts? I mean, about Jesus?"

Stone, ever honest and childlike in his faith, said, "Not really. Not too much. I lived my early years without Jesus, and He made such a huge change in my life when I got saved that I know He is real." He meant it too. Deliverance from a life of darkness was enough to settle any questions for him.

Ironically, it's not so for a person like me who was born with a Bible in her hand. My daughter's heathen mother spoke: "I do, Grace. All of the time."

She laughed. "But you write Christian books. You play the piano and sing songs at our church. You're always talking to me and Harper and Adelaide about Jesus and praying with us. What do you mean that you have doubts all of the time?"

I explained to her that I don't really doubt Jesus' existence. I've read enough history to know He was real. I've even been to Israel and seen where He lived. The problem for me comes with some of the stuff about Him in the Bible and all of the different ways people interpret it. Sometimes I can get wacky and question a lot of things.

A light flickered in her eyes when I said this. "That's me. I mean, I do believe in Him. I just wish I didn't doubt. It makes me feel bad; I don't want to be this way. I want to be strong."

Where'd Grace get the idea she has to be strong? Church? Home? Probably both. It sounds good. But, I'm afraid sometimes we Christians lose sight of what it really means to be strong. Yes, we're told to be strong in the Lord and in the power of His might. But I often need reminding, as my daughter did, that the power has nothing to do with us. Second Corinthians 12:9 says that His grace is sufficient for us, and His power—His strength—is made perfect in our weakness.

We talked about the Scripture where the father of a sick child says to Jesus, "Lord, I believe; help Thou my unbelief" (Mark 9:24 KJV). I told Grace that's where I live, and I'm learning to accept that it's okay. God is big enough for our doubts. In fact, our weakness just gives Him another opportunity to show His power.

Her daddy and I may have different stories, but we share that same theme: Jesus saved us. He continually saves us. God has demonstrated His love and faithfulness to us over and over. We've seen His power in our lives many times. And she will too, we assured her, as her heart belongs to Him. I could see her little shoulders relaxing. She curled up beside us and went to sleep.

> *Lord Jesus, thank You*
> *for Your patience with me*
> *and for Your faithfulness*
> *even when my faith is weak.*
> *Especially then. My heart belongs*
> *to You. Your love is amazing!*

Living with the Questions

You will seek me and find me
when you seek me with all of your heart.

JEREMIAH 29:13 NIV

ony and I have been friends since childhood. Our parents taught school together so we had a kinship like some preachers' kids or missionary kids have, or like I suppose any kids do whose parents have the same profession and spend time together. We were always the first ones at school and the last to leave. It seemed like our parents always knew everything. There were kids who picked on us because they didn't like our parents, others who hated us because they thought as teachers' children we got special privileges, and still others who saw it as their duty to make sure we didn't get those special privileges.

Besides being teachers' kids, we also had a lot of other things in common. We were both Christians from an early age, both made good grades, both liked to have fun. When we went to college together at the University of Central Arkansas, we both majored in science, so we had all of the same classes. We studied together almost every night. After college I got married to Stone and Tony went to Optometry School in Memphis. But over the years we've managed to stay in touch, and he's like a second uncle to my kids.

Last year Stone and I went to see Tony in Dallas, where he is an optometrist. There was a U2 concert in the new Dallas Cowboys stadium, and the three of us went. We had a ball, waving and singing along with Bono from the nosebleed section. Like always, we also stayed up late talking about spiritual things.

Tony told me about a class he'd been taking at his church called, "Living with the Questions." Like me, he struggles at times with reconciling what he thinks in his head and what he feels in his heart. I felt inspired by the name of the class, and the premise, which seemed to be that it's okay to ask questions in faith, and okay not to have all of the answers.

That's not really normal in the western way of thinking. Just like we typically want all stories to have happy endings, we want all of our questions to be answered. It's like there's this fear that unanswered questions threaten what we believe. It's like not knowing is a weakness. It shows something lacking in our faith, or worse, seems to raise the possibility that there's something lacking in our God. But nothing could be further from the truth. He's big enough for our questions—and big enough that we'll never be able to answer them all, at least till we get to heaven.

As I grow in my relationship with Christ, seeking the answers to specific questions grows less and less important. However, seeking Jesus, and living in Him, the one who *is* the answer, grows sweeter and more fulfilling every day. To put it in other words, I am able to be at peace with my questions the more I seek Jesus. He's a great simplifier. Just knowing Him and trying to imitate Him is enough to keep both my mind and heart busy for the rest of my life.

Jesus, be near me as I seek You
with all of my heart—above all else.
Let me not presume that I know
or even can know all of the answers
to my questions. But I know You.
And that's enough.

Are You Sure?

If we confess our sins, he is faithful and just and will forgive us our sins and purify us from all unrighteousness.

1 JOHN 1:9 NIV

The other night Harper got into trouble for aggravating his sisters during teeth-brushing time. During our investigation he got into more trouble for telling a story about it. He got a spanking, and soon after he got hugs and kisses. I sat on the side of the bed to tuck him in and we talked about how honesty is a basic part of trust, how very important it is. I tried to explain to him that the trouble over not telling the truth was worse to me than what he did wrong in the first place.

My little son, who has a tender heart, began to cry.

"Can you forgive me?"

"I always forgive you, and I need you to forgive me too, when *I* make mistakes. Because I do make them. Everyone does—not just you." I always have to throw that in because he tends to take the weight of the world on his small shoulders.

"I still feel really bad inside."

Holding him to me, I suggested maybe he should pray about it, and ask Jesus to forgive Him too.

"What if He doesn't?" He looked up at me, eyes brimming with tears. "Are you sure He will?"

I quoted 1 John 1:9 to him and said that we could count on God's faithfulness. He promises to forgive us, and we can trust that He does. We prayed together and Harper accepted God's forgiveness and laid down to sleep in peace.

I thought about how a child's mind works. Harper's crime was stealing a toothbrush from his sister, just long enough for her to miss it and demand it back. When questioned by the parent police, he denied he did it, compounding the problem. Evidence was produced, and his sentence was a spanking. In his mind's eye, he was a terrible criminal. Could God really forgive him?

It seems silly; so cute and childlike. And yet Harper's response is profoundly telling. It's the same way we adults often approach our relationships with the Lord. We sin, then make the problem worse by trying to cover it up. Conviction sets in, and often guilt. The whole thing makes us feel bad inside and suddenly we feel a great gulf opening up between us and the One who loves us most.

Will He really forgive us? Again? Even for this?

The answer to our questions is the same answer I gave Harper. It's the age-old promise from 1 John. He is *faithful* and *just* to forgive us. He *purifies* us from *all* unrighteousness. All we have to do is ask—He stands ready to forgive and restore us. Like Harper, we can be at peace with Jesus. That is something that can help all of us sleep better at night.

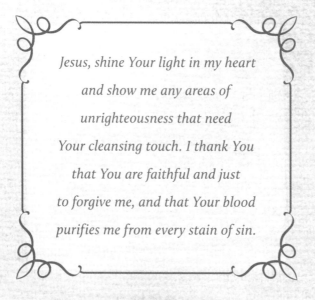

Jesus, shine Your light in my heart and show me any areas of unrighteousness that need Your cleansing touch. I thank You that You are faithful and just to forgive me, and that Your blood purifies me from every stain of sin.

Christianity's Open-Door Policy

I am the door: by me if any man enter in, he shall be saved.

JOHN 10:9 KJV

I attended the Christian Book Expo in Dallas a few years ago. It was a fun experience. Besides signing books and mingling with people in publishing, there were seminars on a range of interesting topics.

My favorite was a debate over New Atheism and Christianity, between Christopher Hitchens and a panel of Christian apologetics led by Doug Wilson and Lee Strobel. For Hitchens, the appearance was part of a book tour across North America to promote his bestseller, a sort of atheist's manifesto. No one could argue that the Oxford-trained debater is less than ingenious as a writer and speaker. His provocative style was entertaining to watch, even though I disagreed with most of what he said.

The format went as follows: A moderator asked a question, and then both sides were given the same amount of time to answer. Scientific facts and historical figures were given. Well-informed, logical opinions were shared. Great thinkers on both sides were quoted. As I sat through the whole debate, my honest assessment was that good arguments were actually presented on both sides. It pleased me that Strobel, probably the leading Christian apologetic in the world, had answers every bit as intellectually compelling as Hitchens.

When time was up, the consensus among many in the audience was that the debate itself was a draw. We all applauded. Then, before dismissal, the moderator, Stan Guthrie, took the liberty of asking a personal question, one that was not scripted. His head involuntarily leaned on one side, and his words were understandable, but slightly slurred. He explained: "I was born with Cerebral Palsy, which is why I talk like this. From the Christian perspective I am valued as a person, and my life has purpose. In fact, even my disability has meaning and what suffering I face finds redemption in Jesus." His voice was humble, seeking. "Mr. Hitchens, I was just wondering. What room is there for me in your belief system?"

At that moment you could have heard a pin drop in the auditorium. I don't even remember the answer Hitchens gave, or if there was one. The point for me was made: In Jesus, the door of grace is open to all. Everyone has purpose. Everyone can step through that door.

That doesn't mean Christopher Hitchens or the other atheists in the room dropped to their knees to receive Jesus. For me, however, it was important. It reminded me of why I believe what

I believe. I can try to prove Christianity is true by studying the Scriptures, reading history, and looking at creation. Someone else can also try to prove it isn't—many have tried, like Hitchens. When we come down to the end of all of the facts, however, there are still many unknowns. I believe we still face a choice. Where do we put our faith?

No other belief system offers the grace, the peace, and the purpose that are found in Jesus. There's simply no one else like Him. He's the answer to our most difficult questions, the provision for our deepest needs. And He offers Himself freely—not just to the elite. Not just the fittest. He's the door that's wide open to life everlasting. In Jesus, there's room for everyone.

> *Thank You, Jesus, for being the door*
> *that leads to the kingdom of God,*
> *both on earth and in heaven.*
> *In You, anyone can find value, purpose,*
> *meaning, and redemption. Even me!*
> *Your grace truly is amazing!*

The Best Thing

I am with you always.

MATTHEW 28:20 NIV

Last fall we Faulkenberrys took a trip to Europe to see a good friend of ours named Ruston who lives in Munich. It was quite an adventure, to say the least, with three small children. Stone and I had to modify our *Amazing Race* style traveling, as in the past we've tried to see everything a place has to offer in short amounts of time. Thank goodness our friend had a cozy apartment where we were able to crash between excursions. Because of Munich's location and his gracious hospitality, we were still able to take our kids to see many marvelous things.

There's a fantasy-like castle located in Bavaria called Neuschwanstein. Everybody loved it because going inside is like stepping into a Disney movie and becoming a fairytale character. We also went to Rothenburg on the Tauber River, where Harper got to pretend he was back in the days of Robin Hood. Together we walked almost completely around the village on an intact medieval wall, peering through slits carved for arrows and imagining what it would be like to see the enemy advancing on horseback and foot.

Fulfilling Grace's dream took us on an overnight train to Amsterdam, so she could see the Anne Frank House. It was special and bittersweet to watch her enter Anne's room with its movie star pictures on the wall. I believe such an experience changes one forever. We also took in the beauty of that city, with its dreamy canals, art museums, and thousands of bicyclers.

Back home in Arkansas, we looked at pictures and discussed with our family what the highlights of the trip were. Adelaide was asked first what she enjoyed most, and she said, "Being at Ruston's house and eating happy cherries!" (This was a candy our friend bought for her.)

Harper's answer was about the same: "I really liked all of it, but my favorite thing was being with Ruston."

"That was the best part to me too," Grace chimed in.

Stone and I looked at one another and laughed. We had spent our savings to take our kids halfway around the world, and the best thing to them about the whole trip was being with our friend in his apartment. What's more, we had to agree that being with Ruston as a family was our favorite part too!

It seems that wherever you are, and whatever you're doing, it's who is with you that makes the difference. Of course it was awesome for our family to go on a vacation to Germany. But what was best about it was not the wonderful places we went, but the time we got to enjoy with Ruston (and each other).

That's just like our journey through life. We have great days and beautiful experiences—those are even better with Jesus near us. And when things are difficult, it's His presence that sees us through. He's also in all of the in-between spaces, the daily living. Even mundane things can be infused with purpose when we consider He is with us. Jesus' presence is one thing we can always count on, wherever we go. He is with us. And that's by far the best thing about life on earth.

Jesus, thank You for always being near me wherever I go. You are the air I breathe and the still, small voice within me, whispering words of Your care.

Is God in Here?

Where can I go from your Spirit? Where can I flee

from your presence? If I go up to the heavens, you are there;

if I make my bed in the depths, you are there. If I rise on the wings

of the dawn, if I settle on the far side of the sea, even there

your hand will guide me, your right hand will hold me fast.

PSALM 139:7–10 NIV

Adelaide, now four, has been asking a lot of questions about God lately. I can see the little wheels turning inside her head as she ponders the things she's learning at Granny and Pa Pa's house (otherwise known as "school"), church, and home. For example, the other night in bed she raised up, just out of the blue, and asked, "Is God in this bed with us?"

We laughed and said yes. He's everywhere.

Down at the beach, we were walking together on the sand. She picked up a shell, examining it carefully, and then held it up to me, "Is God in here?"

This was a first. But after a little consideration, I answered, "Yes, Adelaide, He's everywhere."

Even today in the car going down the road, she asked me, "Is God in this car, Mommy?" And when I answered, "Yes, of course," she said, "Am I sitting on His lap?"

I don't know exactly what is going on with my child, but I suspect she may be wondering, as I have a tendency to do sometimes, if God ever *isn't* in a place. Is there anywhere we can go that He won't tag along?

A friend of mine tells a story about the time she found out her husband had lung cancer. Like it would most of us, the diagnosis sent her reeling, grasping for the faith she had long held very dear. She wondered if she could still trust in the Lord's goodness... His faithfulness...His provision. Her faith was tested in the light of such news.

She said she was ironing one day when she came to the moment of truth. The question presented itself: *Do you believe there are any cracks in My love?* And the answer that came from deep in her spirit, surprising even to her, was: *No. I know there are no cracks in Your love.*

My friend is a spiritual giant in my eyes, and yet her story is much the same as Adelaide's, isn't it? Stone and I have taught our daughter God is everywhere, always. She believes us, but then she gets in a certain situation and the questions assail her. In the bed: "Is He here?" Looking at a seashell: "Could He really be here too?" In the car: "What about here? Even here?"

It seems we all need to be reminded of the answer from time to time. *He is here.* Jesus will never leave us nor forsake us. There is no place we can get away from Him, no crack or imperfection in His love.

Wow, Jesus, You really are everywhere. Help me remember that. Nothing escapes Your notice, and I am never outside Your loving care. When questions come, give me the faith to say from my spirit: Nothing can separate us. There are no cracks in Your love.

Love Your Chother

If we love each other, God lives in us,
and his love is made perfect in us.

1 JOHN 4:12 NCV

My youngest daughter Adelaide and her cousin Sophia are ten months apart. We joke that Sophia provided the inspiration for Adelaide, and it is basically true. Stone and I had been thinking about having another baby, and when we held the cute little bundle that was Sophia in our arms for the first time, she sort of sealed the deal. We knew we wanted to give her another little cousin to love.

The "babies," as they are called in our family, are definitely buddies. As I write this they are three and four years old and almost like twins—completely inseparable. Sophia's mother and I both went to work this year, after being stay-at-home moms for several years, and Sophia and Adelaide entered an elite private preschool called River Bluff Academy (otherwise known as Pa Pa and Granny's house). It is just through the woods from our houses and run by my parents, a retired teacher and principal. Sophia and Adelaide are the only students. Needless to say, they get lots of one-on-one attention.

The babies have created their own games to play and developed much of their own language through the years. One game they love to play is "Friend." In this game they visit each other's houses with their baby dolls and have a tea party. If they have their way, "tea" in the form of water flows freely, along with grapes, blueberries, strawberries, and Nilla Wafers. (Sometimes they must settle for wooden food.) Then they take their dolls for a stroll outside on the deck. Their days at "school" are a combination of rigorous academics overseen by Granny and Pa Pa and games like "Friend." They may fuss with each other occasionally, but then they get right back to loving and playing. It's so fun to watch. They each call the other one their "best."

Not long ago a stomach virus made the rounds in our respective households. Trying to keep everybody apart, I stayed home while my kids were sick, and then René stayed home with hers. Almost a week went by without the babies being together. On the day that Adelaide felt better, she cried to go see Sophia, who was still infirm.

"Mommy, I haven't seen Sophia in a lot of days. She's

my best. She misses me. We need we's chother. We love we's chother!"

She's my best. We need we's chother. We love we's chother.

Meditating on those adorable words, I glimpsed a simple truth about the kingdom of heaven. We need each other. The Bible says if we love each other, God lives in us, and His love is made perfect in us. It's that easy and that hard. But if we want God living in us, perfecting us in His love, then we have to love other people. Like Sophia and Adelaide, we were designed to love we's chother.

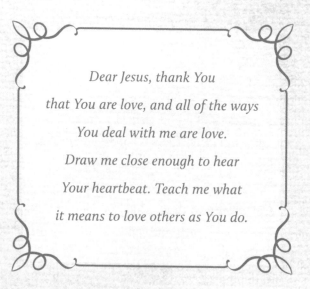

Dear Jesus, thank You
that You are love, and all of the ways
You deal with me are love.
Draw me close enough to hear
Your heartbeat. Teach me what
it means to love others as You do.

What Calvary Said

A new command I give you: Love one another.

As I have loved you, so you must love one another.

By this everyone will know that you are my disciples,

if you love one another.

JOHN 13:34–35 NIV

From time to time I direct the choir at church in a seasonal musical production. On one particular occasion we were working on an Easter musical called *The King is Coming*, which consisted of several songs sung by the choir and an accompanying drama that involved little kids. I practiced with the choir each week and then held separate practices with the cast for several weeks until, the last week before Easter, we put the two groups together.

As inevitably happens in a production of this magnitude, there were stressful moments. Church is just a group of fallible people, after all. The cliché fits: Christians aren't perfect, just forgiven. Often we get to practice that forgiveness God has shown us with each other. We experience conflicts of interest. In the case of this musical, I'm sure I may have disappointed people and gotten on a few nerves. The atmosphere was not always Easterly. Several times I went home a little frustrated (or a lot). However, for better or worse, we all—choir, cast, and crew—stuck together till the end.

The songs in the musical were beautifully written, and on the night of the performance, a peace came over me, re-minding me just to relax and let the Spirit flow. I'd done all I could do in terms of elbow grease—we all had—and it was time to let go and let the message of the once and future King Jesus shine.

We flew through the first several numbers. It always goes faster when you're not stopping to correct mistakes. Then we came to a song called *Written in Red*. It's really slow, and a line that repeats over and over in it is this: "'I love you. I love you.' That's what Calvary said."

As I listened to those words and drank them in, letting them seep deep down into my bones, the miracle of Easter came to me personally. I suddenly felt warm all over. He loves me. *He loves me.* It's like the riddle people say while picking petals from a flower, except that there's no *He loves me not*.

No possibility of that, because of Calvary, because of the cross.
He loves me. That's what Calvary said.

> *Jesus, You know better than anyone*
> *that love is sometimes tough.*
> *But You never give us a command*
> *without supplying the power it takes*
> *to obey. I desire to do Your will.*
> *I desire to love others as You love,*
> *so that people can see*
> *and know that I am Your disciple.*

Broken and Beautiful

We also glory in our sufferings,
because we know that suffering produces perseverance;
perseverance, character; and character, hope.

ROMANS 5:3–4 NIV

A few years ago I met a lady named Sandy Terry. I was actually having a really bad day when she called me up out of the blue and introduced herself. Turns out she had read one of my books and it blessed her. She felt led to call and let me know and so she did, providing specific examples of how the book had touched her heart. It was a great encouragement.

After that, we agreed to meet for lunch at a little coffee shop. I asked her lots of questions to get to know her, as she did me. I found out that she lost her mother to breast cancer, and battled it herself. Her life seemed to exemplify the above verse. She absolutely exuded hope.

I've had the opportunity to meet with Sandy semi-regularly, and certain themes have emerged from our conversations. The first is that though she may have learned something from one of my books back in the day, I am primarily her student in the school of faith. The second is the bigger lesson: the beauty of brokenness.

Yesterday we had lunch and somehow started talking about our personal church histories. She told me about her journey from one denomination to the other in search of a deeper Christian life. Just as they did when she first told me about the cancer, her eyes lit up as she described what sounded to me like harsh and harrowing experiences. Under His discipline, God has allowed her to be crushed into pieces—both physically and spiritually—so that He might put her together again as a new creation. He took the pieces of her pain—her loss, her physical pain, her moments of doubt and fear—and fashioned them into a beautiful soul who now has the capacity to encourage and mentor people like me.

It's a beautiful thing, and a deep mystery to me, when someone like Sandy speaks of such suffering as a gift of grace. God has applied His severe mercy in her life in a way I'd never ask for, and yet in her eyes I see something so valuable I almost covet it. Almost.

I think what one sees in Sandy is the same thing we see

at the cross, for there is unspeakable beauty in brokenness. Jesus, the Son of God, was broken and His blood spilled to secure our hope, our future glory. He was allowed to suffer so that He could offer us a life of eternal beauty. May we look to Him as our example when things come along to break us. Like Sandy, may we accept them as gifts of grace, pieces of the puzzle of our life that will one day fit together into something beautiful.

Jesus, You were broken for me.
Thank You that as I encounter suffering,
it is an opportunity to identify with You,
to grow deeper in my faith,
to know You better. Help me find
Your beauty in my brokenness.

Peanuts

With men it is impossible, but not with God:
for with God all things are possible.

MARK 10:27 KJV

My parents have a brown paper sack in their pantry that is full of raw peanuts. When it gets empty, my dad goes to the Farmer's Cooperative in town and buys another one. It's a family tradition to roast them in the oven and eat them hot, but we also eat them right out of the bag. The grandkids especially like to grab a handful. For as long as I can remember, we have rarely gone without peanuts in my parents' house.

Adelaide stays with my parents Monday through Thursday while I am teaching at the university. It is her own private "school" which she shares with her cousin, Sophia. After work is over, it is not uncommon for me to walk into their home to pick

Adelaide up and find her in the recliner on my father's lap eating peanuts. They are usually watching *Little Bear* or *Franklin* on the television. I like to sit down and visit.

The other day I came in and Adelaide was still napping with her Granny and Sophia in the "big bed" in my parents' bedroom. My dad was in the living room, enjoying a short reprieve from Nickelodeon, and I sat down with him to watch *Headline News*. As if on cue, Adelaide woke up and padded down the hall to greet us. She gave me a hug, and then proceeded into the kitchen where I heard her rustling around in the pantry. She came back into the living room with a small wooden bowl full of peanuts. She climbed into her Pa Pa's lap.

I saw Adelaide work on a peanut, trying to crack it with her tiny fingers. When the shell wouldn't budge, she resorted to using her teeth.

"Don't use your teeth on them," my dad told her.

"I can't crack 'em, though." She set down the peanut. Then she handed the bowl to him.

He gave her a questioning look.

"I can't crack 'em, Pa Pa, but you can."

They turned the channel from *Headline News* to *Sponge Bob* and my dad cracked the peanuts. As he cracked each one, he handed it to Adelaide who ate them one by one.

Besides being adorable, and filling my heart with utter joy, this simple interaction was a perfect illustration to me of how God works in our lives. We try to do something ourselves and it's beyond our power. Either the peanut won't crack at all, or we try to force it with our teeth and end up getting hurt, or at the very least, make a terrible mess. Then by His grace the thought occurs to us: *I can't do this, but He can.* We set the problem or need in His lap. Never once does He consider rejecting us or forcing us to go it alone. He simply takes whatever we offer, and with able hands He works it out in His perfect will, His perfect way, His perfect time. All we have to do is hold out our hands and wait.

> *Lord Jesus, there is so much I can't do,*
> *but You can. In this moment I'm placing*
> *everything before You, to sort out,*
> *to fix what's broken, to make all things*
> *beautiful in Your time, Your will,*
> *Your way. Thank You that I can rest*
> *in Your arms. Thank You that You are*
> *able—and willing—to help me.*

Don't Worry, Be Trusting

Therefore I tell you, do not worry about your life....
Who of you by worrying can add a single hour to his life?

MATTHEW 6:25, 27 NIV

I am the mother of a very boyish little boy who is eight years old. Despite my efforts to steer him in the direction of culture and art, his primary interests in life are fishing and hunting. Our daily routine consists of school, piano and guitar practice after school, minimal homework, and then adventure till dark.

"Adventure till dark" might not sound so bad, if the image it conjures is a fenced-in back yard with a tree house and swing set. But our back yard—and the front yard too, for that matter— is wild wilderness. Our house sits on a five-hundred-foot high bluff above the Arkansas River in the middle of the woods.

We share those woods with all kinds of wildlife. Harper likes to take his BB gun along when he goes adventuring, and in recent developments has acquired a little four-wheeler he likes to drive by himself. His dream—not to be realized any time soon—is to drive himself several acres away to the pond we call *Lake Adelaide,* and fish out of a kayak. He'd like to clean the fish he catches with his own sharp pocketknife, but I tell him that's not happening either. At least not till he's in college.

When we first got the four-wheeler, it had a remote kill switch. I enjoyed the power and security of sitting on the porch, watching, remote in hand. If Harper ever went dangerously fast, I could turn off the engine from the comfort of my wicker rocker. It was lovely.

However, now that he has gained experience and proven himself as a driver, the remote seems a little excessive. A little controlling. He's eight, after all. Not five. And I am well aware that little boys—and girls too—need space to grow. If I want Harper to become a responsible adult, I have to give him responsibilities that are age-appropriate as he grows. And I have to trust him.

To do that, I have to trust Jesus with him. I want to be wise and responsible, but within those boundaries, I also have to give up my false sense of control. Like Jesus taught, worrying gets us nowhere. We need to listen to His voice to guide us in making good decisions, but beyond that, all of life is an exercise in trust.

I read once that Brennan Manning asked a friend of his to sum up the Christian life in a few words. His friend said he could do it in one word: *trust.* Whether it's our family, our jobs, or anything else in our lives, we need to make that word our mantra.

> *Jesus, sometimes it is so hard*
> *for me to trust, even though*
> *I know I should. I'm laying*
> *all of my worries at Your feet now.*
> *By Your mercy and power,*
> *help me not to pick them back up.*

Family Matters

My true brother and sister and mother
are those who do what God wants.

MARK 3:35 NCV

*E*veryone I know experiences family conflict on some level, whether directly or indirectly. And for the person who desires to follow Christ, sometimes this issue can become convoluted in a labyrinth of seemingly contradictory teaching—from the Bible itself as well as from respected Bible teachers. *Turn the other cheek. Shake the dust from your feet. Honor thy father and mother. He who would follow Me must hate his mother and father. Forgive and forget. Reconcile. As much as lies within you, live at peace....*

As with everything we face as Christians, God deals with us personally and individually. What works in one family may not work in another. There are so many variables among families—how we deal with our own must be directed by the Spirit. And we need not judge others who think differently than we do.

I came across something the other day that helped increase my understanding of Jesus' perspective on this dilemma. While I've studied a lot about His teachings, I've not thought a great deal about his dealings with His own family. Mary and Joseph are figures that fade in my mind after the nativity, with Mary appearing again for support at the crucifixion. I know John the Baptist was his cousin, and I knew he had siblings, but I guess I've never focused on that fact. The Bible doesn't say a whole lot about them.

While that lack of information in itself may be important (absence and silence can sometimes speak volumes about a relationship), there's a passage in Mark that offers a few clues as to how Jesus dealt with difficulties in His family. Mark 3 tells us Jesus was ministering to a crowd of people, and the place got so full that He and His disciples were not able to eat. When His family heard about this (note that they were not there), they came to try to "take charge of Him for, they said, 'He is out of His mind'" (v. 21 NIV). Jesus, of course, does not stop what He is doing, and when someone tells Him His family has arrived, He looks around the crowded room and points to the group that is gathered. "Here are my mother and brothers! Whoever does God's will is my brother and sister and mother" (vv. 34–35 NIV).

In the example of Jesus, I don't see disrespect. I also don't see an effort to force His family into His belief system, or His mission. What I do see is that He answers a higher call than what their will is, and that His self-knowledge triumphs over what they think of Him. I see that He is misunderstood. I also see that this doesn't get in the way of His calling. Finally, I see that He embraces the others God has given Him as His family—the family of God—and He continues to pour His life into them.

Oh Jesus, as in all things,
help me imitate You
as I interact with my family.

Rich and Poor

"Truly I tell you," he said, , "this poor widow has put in more than all the others. All these people gave their gifts out of their wealth; but she out of her poverty put in all she had to live on."

LUKE 21:1–4 NIV

I love the old movie *It's a Wonderful Life* with Jimmy Stewart. My favorite moment in the movie (besides the time when the dancers fall in the swimming pool) comes at the very end, when all of the people George has helped through the years show up at his house to give him aid. They shower him with money to bail him out of his bind, but most of all the viewer is shown how much George means to each one of the townspeople. His brother Harry proposes a toast: "To my brother George, the richest guy in town!"

I can remember my dad saying the same thing of our family, growing up, and I would question him. "Us? Rich? I don't think so." We had a nice house and clothes, and plenty of food to eat, but we certainly weren't the richest people in town. Not even close. The richest people were the bankers, lawyers, and doctors. People in the oil and gas business. Certainly not the teachers.

My dad would just smile at me. "We are rich in everything that is important."

The kingdom of God could also be called the kingdom of reversals. The King of it all was born in a stable. He told us the first would be last and the last first. It also seems that those richest by kingdom standards are sometimes the poorest people in the world. Consider the widow in Luke's story who gave all she had. She only gave two copper coins, but her act of sacrifice made her rich in Jesus' approval.

On Valentine's Day this year I scurried from class to class and then to lunch. When I returned to my office from lunch I noticed my door was decorated with a balloon. There was a pot of hyacinths on the floor, infusing the hallway with a lovely scent. A coffee cup and card were set beside it. Who could have done it? I knew Stone could not have been there; besides, he had already spoiled the kids and me that morning before school and work.

Opening the card, I found that it was from a student. One of my past pupils, a single mom who struggles to make ends meet. The previous semester I'd walked with her to the parking lot every Thursday after night class because some creep was stalking her. I knew she didn't have a dime. And yet she remembered I like coffee. And fresh flowers. There was even candy—for my kids, the card said—with the balloon.

I sat down at my desk and cried. I've never given from the standpoint of poverty. Perhaps I've known poverty of spirit—or at least energy—and kept giving at times. But as Beth Moore puts it in her study on Esther, I am "woefully rich in all things self." God used this student, like the widow and her coins, to remind me of what's valuable in His kingdom. A heart that gives out of all she has.

Jesus, I want to give out of all
that is in me—everything I have is Yours.
Guide me, today, to some need
I may fill, out of the glorious
riches of Your kingdom.
And help me not to hold back.

Faithful and True

Now I saw heaven opened, and behold, a white horse.
And He who sat on him was called Faithful and True.

<small>REVELATION 19:11 NKJV</small>

One semester I had a woman in one of my classes who was very young, very bright, and very tough. Through writing exercises such as "Describe Your Childhood Home" and observations she shared in class, I deduced that her life had not been very easy.

She was the child of alcoholic parents. She grew up in poverty. She moved out on her own in her teens, and had been betrayed by virtually every person she should have been able to trust. The message life's experiences had ingrained in her was this: *Everyone is against you. Trust no one. You have to take care of yourself.* It was obvious she followed this motto. She now had fought her way into college, and she was none too eager to trust me.

I remember the first time I realized the depth of her distrust. I gave an assignment, and she was absent that day. When she came to my office later to talk to me about it, she practically threatened bodily harm if I did not accept her make-up work.

"Whoa, whoa, whoa," I said, inviting her to sit down. "Why so hostile?"

She instantly burst into tears. "I know you're very strict about attendance. But I had an emergency."

"Okay," I said. "I make exceptions for emergencies."

The shock that registered on her face was almost comical. "Really? You'll let me turn it in?"

"No problem."

She actually smiled.

I reached out to hug her, and she flinched, so I backed off. I looked her in the eye. "Next time just talk nice to me, okay? A little respect?"

She nodded and turned to leave my office. "Thanks."

As the semester continued, I worked hard to earn her trust. There was no other way to obtain it. Each little kindness I extended was first met with apparent suspicion, then accepted, and sometimes even embraced. By the end of the semester I had gained a friend.

One thing I have prayed for my friend ever since then is that she would open her heart to trust Jesus. Sometimes when we've been wounded by people, it colors our view—not only of other people, but of Jesus. We assign Him the same characteristics of those who let us down, when instead we should judge human behavior by the standard He has set.

I love how Revelation 19:11 describes Jesus as *Faithful and True.* Those aren't only qualities He possesses, however. They are His names. They are *who* He *is.* I am called *Gwen* and *Mommy* and *Mrs. Faulkenberry.* He is called *Faithful and True.* He cannot be unfaithful to us, and He cannot be false. Wow.

Jesus, You're beyond my imagination. There's no one in this world who can compare to You. Help me not to think of You in terms of human imperfection, but as the One who is Faithful and True. Thank You that I can trust in You with all of my heart because You will never let me down.

Love Me or Else

Jacob was left alone, and a man wrestled with him till daybreak....

Then the man said, "Let me go, for it is daybreak."

But Jacob replied, "I will not let you go unless you bless me." ...Then he

blessed him there. So Jacob called the place Peniel, saying,

"It is because I saw God face to face, and yet my life was spared."

GENESIS 32:24, 26, 29–30 NIV

The story of Jacob wrestling with God is a mind-bender. I'll admit I don't understand everything about it. But that doesn't stop me from thinking it's really cool, and speculating as to what in the world went on there.

This story was quickened in me one night as I was talking with a friend. She was a student of mine who attended a Bible study I led in my home before I had kids. It was affectionately called WOGs, short for Women of God.

The Women of God consisted of girls from all kinds of

different backgrounds. This particular girl was struggling with drugs and feeling very distant from God.

"When I pray I don't feel anything. It's just like I'm mouthing words. How do I know He's really listening?"

"Sometimes God is like the wind. We can't see the wind, but when it moves through the leaves they quiver. We know the wind is there."

"I wish He would move through me. I'm trying. Spiritually, though, nothing is happening."

This is the moment the thought of Jacob came to me.

"Do you remember the story of Jacob wrestling with God?"

Being raised in Sunday school, she did.

"Do you remember what happens in that story?"

"Well, as I remember it was kind of weird."

"I think so too, and I don't understand it all, but there's one part where God says He wants to go, and Jacob says, 'I will not let you go unless you bless me.'"

She remembered.

"Maybe that's what you need to do. Wrestle with God over these doubts you're having. Keep praying and seeking Him. Don't let Him go until He blesses you."

I believe one thing that can be gleaned from the story of Jacob wrestling with God is that God honors a tenacious faith. One that won't let go, even when it doesn't make sense. The "man" blessed Jacob when Jacob clung to Him. Jacob knew there was a blessing coming. And it was worth whatever wrestling it took to receive it.

Franz Wright wrote a poem called "Request" that reminds me of the story of Jacob wrestling with the angel. The last line of the poem speaks volumes: "Love me or else."

To me, this poem affirms tenacious faith. The poet recognizes He doesn't have anything to offer God—he compares his poetry to a song played on a toy guitar. But He requests to be loved, like Jacob, in a "must have it" sort of way. I believe it pleases God when we must have His love—His blessing—or else. That's a faith that recognizes His value, and the fact that without Him, all of our wrestling is meaningless.

Jesus, be near me today. I need You, I long for You, I must have You in my life. Without You, I am lost. I am desperate for Your touch today, and I trust that You stand ready to give it. Like Jacob, I will not let You go unless You bless me.

The Greatest Miracle

If you confess with your mouth the Lord Jesus and believe in your heart
that God has raised Him from the dead, you will be saved.
For with the heart one believes unto righteousness,
and with the mouth confession is made unto salvation.

ROMANS 10:9–10 NKJV

One Sunday, a lady named Lois was asked to give her testimony during the church service. I'd known her for about a year, ever since she and her husband moved to Ozark and started attending our church. In that year, we'd been together in choir some, and I'd talked to her at church socials. She likes animals and raises goats, like I do, so besides Jesus and church, we had that in common.

I was not prepared for the impact of her testimony. She stood in front of the church, really nervous, this totally normal-looking middle-aged woman. Then she proceeded to tell us how she'd been raised in an abusive home and led a pretty rough life as an adult until one day a neighbor knocked on her door.

Lois was new in town, and didn't know the neighbor lady from Eve. The lady invited her to church and, surprisingly, Lois went. She heard the gospel of Jesus there and received Him as her personal Savior. Since then He has totally changed her life.

I was spellbound by Lois' story, even though it's an old one. Or perhaps I should say, *because* it's an old one. You don't hear a lot of stories like that anymore. At least in my circle of friends, a person's "coming to Jesus" experience usually happens more in the context of an established relationship.

It happens sometimes with my students. Most of them come into my class as strangers. As the semester unfolds, I look for opportunities to minister to their needs, which mostly means listening to them when they seek me out to talk, sometimes sharing a meal with them, praying for and sometimes with them. Of course not every student has a life-changing experience as a result of my class. But if God chooses to use me in some of their lives, and the Spirit moves in their hearts to respond, then it can be really cool. I guess this process is what a seminary student might call my "style of evangelism." I just believe it's the way God wired me.

What was so neat about listening to Lois' story was that the Lord reminded me that He uses all kinds of "styles" to get

His purpose accomplished. Lois was for real. *This really happens,* I found myself thinking. *This really still happens to people. It happened to Lois.*

How refreshing that everyone is not called to be the same, or to minister in the same way. We all have different gifts. But the greatest miracle of all time is that Jesus comes to people. It may be through a relationship or it may be through a stranger's knock on the door. Being open to sharing His gospel whenever—and however—He sees fit enables us to share in this miracle.

Jesus, I thank You that You live in me. Thank You for the people and circumstances You use to draw me to Yourself. The greatest miracle of my life is that You came to me—and You still come, in the stillness of the morning, in the business of the day, in the dark of night. I want to share this miracle with the world. Use me however You will to lead others to You.

A Forgiven Heart

We know that we belong to the truth and...

we set our hearts at rest in his presence.

1 John 3:19 NIV

We know that when we have unforgiveness in our hearts it quenches the Spirit and makes it hard to feel Jesus is near. But what about when the person we need to forgive is the one in the mirror? My sister-in-law, René, told me she heard a sermon on the importance of forgiveness, based on Matthew 5:7: "Blessed are the merciful: for they shall obtain mercy" (KJV). The speaker told of his own struggles with bitterness and urged the congregation to forgive others. Feeling the Lord was speaking to her heart, she tried to figure out whom she hadn't forgiven.

"I forgave my Dad for being an alcoholic, for never holding a job, for causing us to go hungry," she said, "and I even forgave him for dying and leaving me without a father. I also forgave my mother. I forgave her for being an alcoholic, for being cold to me when I was a child, and for abandoning me."

Who was left? She could not figure out who remained unforgiven in her heart.

"The speaker asked us to think of who it is that pops into our head during prayers," she told me. "It was in that moment that the answer fell into place. God revealed to me the one I still desperately needed to forgive. *Me*."

Growing up, René secretly blamed herself for her family's problems. She and her brother did not deserve the things that happened to them and couldn't control the situation. Even so, in her heart there was a little piece of the blame hidden away.

"As a young woman, I made mistakes. I was needy and reached out to the wrong people, making bad choices. Shame was never far from me.

"Once I became a Christian, I was a new creation. But was I really? Could someone like me be made clean? I remained skeptical on that point."

Even after the amazing blessings of marriage and motherhood, René blamed herself when things went wrong. "I had a miscarriage. I immediately thought it was my fault—it had to be," she explained.

She felt she deserved the depression that followed. "What I

did not deserve was the beautiful family and life," she admintted. "It was somehow my fault that my little baby died in my body."

One month after her baby would have been born, she sat in church, faced with the question of whom she still needed to forgive. "Clearly, it was me."

"I threw myself on the mercy of God, asking Him to help me forgive myself," René confided. "I finally gave Him all of the guilt, shame, and secrets that kept me from hearing the truth about His love and acceptance."

René's story stays with me as I live my own life and offer counseling to others. It is important to remember His mercy extends to each of us. Personally. His forgiveness is great enough to cover our sins and cleanse our hearts.

Jesus, thank You that because of Your death on the cross, my sins and my shame are washed away. I receive the truth of Your love and forgiveness. My past has no power over me because of You!

Ouch—I Mean, Thank You!

Wounds from a friend can be trusted, but an enemy multiplies kisses.

PROVERBS 27:6 NIV

Not long ago I turned in a devotional manuscript to my editor. I thought it was great, fresh, and most of all, inspired. She sent it back to me with notes like, "You make a good point, but this is not appropriate for a devotional book," and "People who pick up a devotion are not looking for a critique of contemporary Christianity. They are looking for encouragement. Please revise."

My first reaction was hurt. The sting of rejection. As is typical, hurt feelings soon segued into a bit of indignation and the desire to defend myself. At that point, thank the Lord, His Spirit stepped in to remind me of past experiences I've had down that road. It never seems to take me where I want to go. So I took a deep breath, whispered a prayer, and stepped back to reconsider the situation.

As I opened my heart and mind to what Jesus might have to say to me in my disappointment, two things became evident. One was hope. *Nothing is wasted with Me*, I felt Him say. *Trust Me with your work.* The other thing He reminded me was that my editor is my friend. We have a wonderful history together. She is a person who I know loves the Lord and practices kingdom principles in her job. She is not my enemy—we are on the same side.

This second point rang crystal clear as we spoke on the phone later that day. I set myself to receive her words because they were the words of a friend. And even though they wounded, she was right. Her words were to be trusted. I was able to learn something from them that I believe will help me to grow both as a person and a writer. Wounds from a friend produce healing.

How much more so do the words of our Lord bring us from sickness into health, death into life. It wounds me to be told "love your neighbor" when that neighbor doesn't love me. It wounds me to hear the words "forgive—seventy times seven" when the first few times were difficult enough. And it wounds me to know He wants me to deny myself daily, pick up my cross, and follow Him. These are not easy words to receive.

But the Bible also says, "Greater love has no man than this, that He lay down His life for His friends" (John 15:13 NIV). We'll never find a better friend than Jesus. And His words, even when they wound, can be trusted. After all, "To whom shall we go? [He has] the words of eternal life" (John 6:68 NIV).

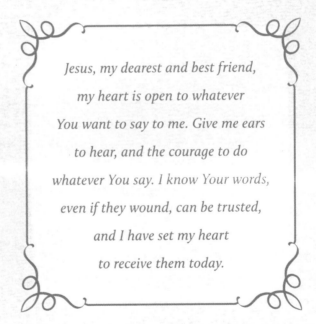

Jesus, my dearest and best friend, my heart is open to whatever You want to say to me. Give me ears to hear, and the courage to do whatever You say. I know Your words, even if they wound, can be trusted, and I have set my heart to receive them today.

Prized Possessions

For God so loved the world that he gave his one and only Son,

that whoever believes in him shall not perish but have eternal life.

JOHN 3:16 NIV

It was close to Mother's Day and the children of our church, under the direction of their wonderful SWAT (Service With Actions Team) leaders, had been working on a surprise for all of the women. For several weeks, I would take my kids every Sunday evening and drop them off at SWAT under a shroud of secrecy. They insisted I not linger. It was important to them that I not see their handiwork and ruin the surprise.

When Mothers' Day came the kids were very excited. I was sitting in my Sunday school class with other ladies when the SWAT team knocked on the door. Several children poured in with handmade gifts and distributed them to everyone. No woman was left out, even the ones who weren't mothers. The

SWAT team had made things for all of the ladies in general, and gave hugs all around.

Adelaide, however, only had eyes for me. She made a beeline to where I was sitting. Her gift was not a "general" gift, but the package was labeled, *To Mommy, From Adelaide*, and she held it out as though it was her most prized possession. In that moment it was. And so it would become for me.

Tearing off the wrapping, I unpacked a small flowerpot that had been painted silver. Around the top was glued a piece of lace, and to accent the lace, a metallic gold ribbon. In one spot, a shiny, hot pink bunny was pressed into the center of the ribbon.

The inside of the pot was stuffed with silk flowers of every color imaginable. There were tiny bundles of roses in purple, red, white, orange and black. Down the sides of the pot were glued further varieties of flowers: orange, lavender and pink. A purple bow was added, and silk leaves were sprinkled throughout.

As I turned it to view from every angle, I was aware of Adelaide's eyes on me. She waited and watched, expectantly, for my reaction. I touched each blossom and told her it was the most beautiful flowerpot I had ever seen. Then I enfolded her in a hug and she said, "Happy Mothers' Day Mommy!"

Now the flowerpot sits on my desk, near an exquisite box a friend brought me from Italy. A picture of Emily Dickinson had to go in order to make room. Every time I look at Adelaide's creation, a lump rises in my throat. It is one of my most prized possessions and I show it off to everyone who comes by. What makes it so special is that my four-year-old Adelaide gave her all—for me.

In a way, it's like what Jesus did for us on the cross. God gave His most prized possession to show His love for us. What pride and tenderness He must feel when He looks at Jesus. And what joy it must bring to His heart when we receive His greatest treasure and share our Savior's beauty with everyone who comes by.

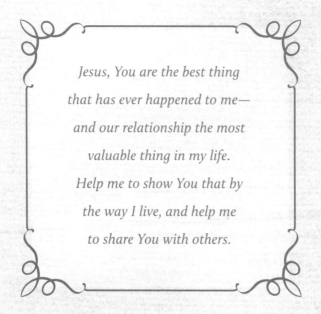

Jesus, You are the best thing that has ever happened to me— and our relationship the most valuable thing in my life. Help me to show You that by the way I live, and help me to share You with others.

Not Only Sovereign

We know that in everything God
works for the good of those who love Him.

ROMANS 8:28 NCV

I was doing fine. Life was going pretty well at home, at work, and even in my writing. Heck, I'd even lost about ten pounds on the low-carb diet! And then all of a sudden it seemed like the edges of my happiness started unraveling. A friend e-mailed that she was diagnosed with breast cancer. Another friend went in for a colonoscopy and two hours later was in surgery for the removal of a tumor the size of a baseball. My aunt had a biopsy that turned out to be malignant. One of my favorite older ladies at our church had a heart attack. Harper had trouble breathing because of asthma. Grace got hit in the nose playing basketball and had to go to the ER. Gas went up to $3.48. A severe storm hit our area. A co-worker's father died.

Another co-worker came back to work, ravaged by the experience of burying her beloved mother, and finding it hard to care about deadlines, schedules, or anything else. We cried together in my office.

Times like this are trying to the soul. Even the soul that believes. Like a spider spinning out threads of silk, we cast about us looking for something to grasp. Words that somehow make sense. An anchor. A place to land. Something—anything—to build our hope on, and in turn to be able to share with others in need.

"God is in control" is a favorite catch-phrase of Christians during these times. "It must be God's will." We simplify pain—our own and other people's—by attempting to put it in a box and labeling it with something that sounds spiritual.

But the gnawing in my gut tells me simple sovereignty is not enough. It brings me no comfort to believe God is in control unless I know something else important about Him. I have to know He is good.

My favorite verse has always been Romans 8:28, for that reason. I can understand that God is in control by the ways He displays His might. From the stories of the Old Testament, like Noah and the Ark and the destruction of Sodom and Gomorrah, to the New Testament when Jesus walks on water, God does amazing things. Powerful things. But what good would it be if He were all-powerful, and yet not all-good?

It's His goodness that makes Him worthy of our trust. It's that logic-defying truth that He is good, even when we can't possibly see how, that enabled Job to say, "Though He slay me, yet will I trust Him" (Job 13:15 KJV). It's the same truth that helped Jesus surrender to the cross. And it's the same truth we can dig our heels into, even when all we see is darkness.

If you are in darkness right now, remember this: God is good. The greatest manifestation of that goodness is that He clothed Himself in human flesh and descended to us as a fragile baby. He walked among us, died for us, and is with us still. Jesus is nearer to you than your next breath. He will never leave you nor forsake you. And He promises—depend upon it— He is working all things together for your good.

Jesus, Your sovereignty and Your goodness transcend my ability to reason. Please give me the grace to trust You completely, no matter what trials I face. Thank You for being near me!

The Crew

His divine power has given us everything we need for a godly life.

2 PETER 1:3 NIV

I've been a Christian since the age of three. I come from a good family, have a happy marriage, and am the mother of three beautiful and talented kids. I have a master's degree. I hold a prestigious teaching position at a university. I am trained in vocal and instrumental music, and I write Christian books.

In Sunday school, people call on me to read because I read fast and can pronounce a lot of words. People call on me to pray because I'm not afraid to pray in public, and I'm told I "pray good." I also sing solos and no one puts their hands over their ears.

Sometimes I'm tempted to think these things matter, that they make me who I am. I sit a little taller in my pew, glancing back at the clock, satisfied. It's then that I see their faces—the ones who remind me of what really matters.

Leaning forward in sincerity with her Bible in her lap is a ninety-two year old woman with an oxygen tank to help her breathe. Another lady sits beside her. She just got off work in time for church, but instead of going home to sleep, she came, thirsty for God's Word. A man sits behind them who has faithfully served as Sunday School Director for over forty years. There. Every. Week. Not because of any leader; he's seen several come and go. Because of Jesus. Because he believes in the cause of a Bible education.

On the next row is a man who plays the harmonica when he's asked. He doesn't read music, he just plays from the heart and makes us cry. Next to him is a couple who ministers weekly to my family. The lady leads my kids in SWAT, which stands for Service With Action Team. She and another woman invest every Sunday night in making sure kids learn to live their faith. Her husband is my husband's friend. He's there whenever we need him, always with a smile.

Behind them is a widower, a genius, an engineer. He speaks both English and Mandarin Chinese and was formerly in the service. And yet he is humble, so meek, so kind. Down the row from him is a lady who decorates the church. She is always behind the scenes making things beautiful. And she's there in her quiet way to support anything anybody ever needs. She holds babies in the nursery, sings in the choir, sends cards when people are sick. She could be the pin-up model for Proverbs 31. I close my eyes. There are more.

As I reflect on this motley little crew called "church," one thing becomes apparent. No pedigree is required for a position in the body of Christ. Many of the ones God uses to touch our church, community, and my life would probably fit in a category called "the least of these." And as I sit in my pew I'm acutely aware: I am not worthy to untie their shoes. Without Him, I am nothing.

> Jesus, You are humble and lowly
> of heart. I want to be like You.
> Help me to be realistic about what
> I truly have to offer. And what I have
> to offer is nothing except You.

Made

I praise you because I am fearfully and wonderfully made.

PSALM 139:14 NIV

*L*ast summer my family participated in Vacation Bible School at our church. Stone told Bible stories, I was a team leader, and all of our kids attended. The way our Bible School program works is that we set up stations, manned by adults and youth, and the team leaders rotate different age groups through each one. The kids go to Bible story, music time, game time, craft time, and everyone's all-time favorite: snack time. My mother is the snack lady.

Several years ago she designed and implemented an incentives program for the children as they work on memorizing Bible verses all week. It's quite sophisticated. She fills a bag with candy bars, and when you say your verse, you get to pick which one you want. It works brilliantly. Even I memorized the verses.

I was the leader for Adelaide's team, the three- and four-year-olds. Actually, I was supposed to be the first grade leader, but Adelaide cried and clung to me the first night, refusing to go to her leader, who is one of the sweetest people in our church. Being the firm disciplinarian that I am, I promptly asked to switch teams with that leader, who was more than happy to move to first grade. My little band of pre-schoolers went from station to station spreading the joys of childhood. Bible story time was especially exciting. Imagine corralling thirteen or so cats into a small space, and then asking them to sit still and listen for about twenty minutes.

All of us were thrilled when it came time for snack time. This particular night, as every night, Mom went all the way around the table, giving each child the opportunity to say his or her verse and get a prize. Several of them belted out: "I am fearfully and wonderfully made!" Their faces glowed triumphantly as they retrieved their Snickers and Kit Kats.

When it was my little cherub's turn, she crossed her arms and shook her head. Apparently, she decided she wouldn't say hers. We'd practiced it at home, and she knew it all right, but it wasn't happening. At least not on command.

Later, when there was no audience, Adelaide pulled my mother to the side. "I know my verse, Granny."

"Okay, Sweetheart, what is it?" Mom knelt down to Adelaide's eye level.

"I want to whisper it in your ear."

Mom leaned over so that Adelaide could cup her ear in her tiny hands.She whispered the words, "I am *made*."

Mom thought she must have heard wrong. "What was that? Can you say it again for Granny?"

Adelaide spoke up, eyes shining. "I. Am. Made!"

Needless to say, she got her candy.

When my mother told me that story we both laughed until our sides hurt. The more I thought about it, however, the more I was compelled by a child's simple understanding, her simple wisdom. My sweet (and ornery) Adelaide left out the adverbs, but she got the gist of the verse. *I'm not an accident or a fluke. I'm not a mistake. You wanted me, designed me, created me. I have a distinct and meaningful purpose. I am* made.

> *Lord Jesus, thank You that all of my days are written in Your book. You know everything about me. Show me the plan that You have for my life, and help me to do Your will, today and every day.*

The Bridge

God is love.

1 John 4:16 KJV

When I was pregnant with our first child, Grace, my beloved Granny was also dying. In fact, she died exactly one month and one day before Grace was born. It was strange to live that experience. Just as one of the most significant people in my life passed out of it, another who would be so significant entered in. I felt, literally, like my body was a bridge. I had one foot in death, and the other in life. And my heart was suspended between those two worlds.

Granny was as close to me as any grandparent could be to a child. We lived just across the pasture from her, and growing up I saw her every day. She cooked dinner for our family every Sunday afternoon. We'd sit around her table after church and visit as she piled on roast beef, mashed potatoes, and homemade yeast rolls, which we drenched in butter and honey.

Like my parents, she was a constant force for good in my life. I have so many memories of being with her, and if I close my eyes, I can still hear her voice. Her blue eyes sparkled with mischief. She liked to go traveling and fishing. She was a giver. A nurturer. A doer. She loved simple things and she knew how to have fun.

So many things about my Granny are woven into the fiber of my being. My stubbornness, my love for life, my curiosity about people. I had hoped to share my own babies with her, so that she could help me love them and teach them about God. I was so sad that they would never know her. Would I be able to tell them everything? Would I remember every detail? That summer, as I mourned Granny's loss even at the birth of my precious daughter, the Lord spoke to my heart out of an unexpected place.

The first few weeks with Grace I spent a lot of time in the recliner. I didn't bother putting her down when she slept; I just held her and studied her perfect features, sometimes taking a nap too. Other times I read some great books. I read a few before I came to *The Bridge of San Luis Rey* by Thornton Wilder. The very ending was a word from God, meant for me that summer. It reads:

"We shall die and all memory of those five [who died in the book] will have left the earth, and we ourselves shall be loved for a while and forgotten. But the love will have been enough; all those impulses of love return to the Love that made them. Even memory is not necessary for love. *There is a land of the living and a land of the dead and the bridge is Love, the only survival, the only meaning.*" [Italics and capitalization of "Love" mine.]

Jesus—our bridge—is our only survival and meaning, especially when tough times come. What a comfort to know He holds our loved ones in His arms, and in faith, we will see them again. It's also a comfort to know that Love—His love, and the love we share in Him—is never lost. It is eternal, and it can never be taken away.

Lord, bathe me in the truth today:
Not that Jesus is like love, or that He
merely gives love, but Jesus is Love.
As His precious ones, Love is in us,
over us, underneath us, around us.
Jesus loves us—and nothing can
ever take that love away.
Thank You, Jesus, for Your love.

I Can't Like It

O the depth of the riches both of the wisdom and knowledge of God!
How unsearchable are his judgments, and his ways past finding out!

ROMANS 11:33 KJV

My brother Jim's best friend Matt is the son of a Methodist preacher. He's married with a family and has a dental practice in northeast Arkansas. The five-hour drive to Cherokee Village, where Matt lives, is too far away from Ozark for Jim's or any of our liking. We still miss the days when Matt would ride his scooter from the Methodist parsonage in the middle of town, up the hill to where our family lived when Jim and I were growing up. They had lots of fun together in those days, and lots of fun pestering me. He will always be like one of the family.

Jim was talking on the phone with Matt one night not long ago when Matt told him a hilarious story. It seems he was trying to teach the song "Jesus Loves Me" to his little daughter, Blakely. Just a few years old, she was having difficulty learning the words.

"I'm tired of this song, Daddy."

Matt recognized her frustration. He tried to encourage her by going more slowly as they focused on the words.

Blakely frowned at him. "I don't like it."

"What do you mean you don't like it?" Matt laughed. "It's a song about Jesus!"

"I don't get it, Daddy." She blinked her big brown eyes. "I *can't* like it."

We thought that was just adorable—so funny, so honest. However, it reminds me of a not-so-funny struggle in my own life.

At times it's hard for me to like God, because I don't always get what He is up to. I see people around me hurting, I see a lot of evil in the world, I see plenty of things that don't make sense. There are questions, relationships, issues in my own life that I still struggle to resolve. Perhaps I always will.

Sometimes, like Blakely, I think I *can't*. I can't be faithful to Jesus; I can't give up my will; I can't trust what I can't see; I can't like—or love—a God I don't always understand. I don't have it in me. I don't have what it takes. I just can't.

This self-doubt would be cause for despair were it not

for a key principle my friend Roy pointed out to me about the kingdom: even though *I* can't, *He* can. Hebrews 2:18 says, "He is able to help us" (NLT). Even if I am faithless, He remains faithful. Even if I withhold trust, He is trustworthy. Even when my feelings betray me, His love is secure. He can—and He promises to—accomplish His perfect will in me.

No, I can't.

But He can.

Jesus, I'll admit I don't always understand You. Like the song says, many of "Your higher ways are not like mine." It's a humbling thing to know I can't. But it also brings great freedom in my life, because You have to supply the power for every moment, every need. I am only a vessel. With You all things are possible. Help me never say, "I can't" without acknowledging that You can.

Abba

For ye have not received the spirit of bondage again to fear;
but ye have received the Spirit of adoption, whereby we cry, Abba, Father.

ROMANS 8:15 KJV

I thought about putting a header across this page that says, "Spoiler Alert." Not because I'm about to reveal any great secret that would spoil the book, but because I myself am what some would call spoiled. Rotten.

I work at my parents' house sometimes when I'm writing. (It's quieter than my house, to put it mildly.) One day I planned to walk over there and work, and I knew my dad would be cooking my breakfast. I've been "doing" the Atkins diet, which my daughter Grace has affectionately dubbed the "bacon diet." Planning for my lunch, I got together a salad and then decided to call my dad.

"Are you cooking breakfast?"

"I sure am."

"Are you making bacon?"

"As we speak."

"Would you mind putting in a few extra pieces that I can eat on a salad later?"

He laughed. "I'd be glad to."

Grace, who was sitting beside me listening to my call, shook her head when I hung up. "Do you mean to tell me your dad is cooking your breakfast *and* lunch?"

"Pretty much."

"How old are you?"

"Thirty-nine and holding."

"You are so beyond spoiled."

I grinned at her. "Kind of like you, huh?"

She held her plate out for her own father to fill it with a stack of his homemade buttermilk pancakes.

I know that not everyone shares this experience, but how I wish we all could. Because, while my dad is not a perfect man, his loving care for me has made it easy-breezy for me to relate to God as my father. It's a natural response.

Some of my earliest memories are of sitting in my daddy's lap, reading books. In the mornings before school, my brother and I used to dress in front of a fire he built for us, and then follow our noses to the kitchen, where he would be cooking homemade cinnamon rolls, ham, or biscuits and gravy.

Before I went off to college, my dad made me learn how to change a flat tire. On again, off again. We sat together in the grass while I practiced. Just in case I ever got stranded and he wasn't there.

A few mornings ago I did get stranded—in my own garage. I called my dad, who lives next door. He didn't reprimand me or give me a speech about irresponsibility. He just said, "I'll be right there." And he was.

I don't mean to over-idealize a human being, or make myself sound like an overgrown child. I am a fairly responsible adult. The point I want to make is that I've seen Jesus—and God the Father—through the love of my dad. When someone actually likes to serve you—enjoys coming to your aid—and wants to protect you—that's love.

Whether or not our fathers have treated us this way, Jesus, You do. You love us. That's why we call You Abba. We reach out to You today. Father.... Daddy.... How we need Your tender love.

Grace's Umbrella

If you then, being evil, know how to give good gifts to your children,
how much more will your Father who is in heaven
give good things to those who ask Him!

MATTHEW 7:11 NKJV

I have always wanted a cool umbrella. I've looked at them in catalogs, the ones that look like a giant flower that unfolds when you open it, or the ones printed with the paintings of my favorite artists. The problem has always been that I am cheap, and the umbrellas that suit my fancy are way too expensive, so I have never sprung for one.

Last year while I was doing some Christmas shopping, I hit the jackpot. For some odd reason, in an unlikely place, I came across a gorgeous umbrella. It had a Monet painting on it just like the umbrellas I've seen in catalogs for thirty or forty dollars. Only this one was seventy-five percent off. I got it for ten dollars! (Merry Christmas to me.)

My umbrella is my prize. I love it. I feel very chic when I walk across the parking lot at work, to my office, or to my class under its Impressionistic shelter.

The other morning it was raining, a cold, biting rain. When René, my sister-in-law, came to pick up the kids up for school Harper gave me a kiss, pulled up the hood on his jacket and dashed to her car. Grace looked at me. "Mommy, can I borrow an umbrella?"

My eyes flashed to the mudroom stand that holds such things as umbrellas and the occasional plastic sword or claw. There was a small, cheap umbrella stashed right beside my awesome one. Perhaps not having all of my wits about me, as it was early, I didn't even hesitate. I grabbed the Monet umbrella and handed it to her. She looked at me like she was surprised, but said, "thanks" and kissed me and headed out the door.

As I watched Grace walk down our sidewalk to René's car, I thought how grown-up she looked under my umbrella. I also thought, with some wistfulness, that I might never see my umbrella—at least not in one elegant piece—again. Such are the facts with ten-year-olds. It surprised even me to realize how easy it had been to hand it to her. Not a thought, really. I would take the little cheap umbrella to work. But my baby got the good one.

I tend, sometimes, to go to God like he's Mr. Scrooge in Dickens' *A Christmas Carol*. "If I could just have this one thing,

Mr. Scrooge, if you wouldn't mind. If it's not too much trouble. I hate to bother you." It's as if He's some miser, up there frowning. But that's my crazy idea, not who the Bible says He really is. God is a gazillion times more giving than I could ever be. I give an umbrella. He gives joy, comfort, life. As much as I love Grace, He loves her so much more. He watches out for all of us, anticipates our needs, and provides for us. He gave me Grace's umbrella to have ready for her before she even asked. He is amazing.

Jesus, this day—this moment—
I'm going to remember the umbrella of
grace that I live under. I'm going
to see You for who You say You are, not
a Scrooge figure, but so much more
generous and loving even than my earthly
father or mother could ever be.
I'm asking You, believing You know my
needs, and am committing myself
to trust You for all good things.

'Tis So Sweet

We trust in the Living God, who is the Savior of all.

1 Timothy 4:10 NKJV

I like old hymns, and one of my favorites is *'Tis So Sweet to Trust in Jesus*. The other day I came across the story behind the writing of it, and it made me like it even more.

It seems Louisa Stead, the woman who wrote it, faced great trials in life. Her husband drowned as she and her daughter watched him attempt to save a drowning child. This was 1875, and his death brought financial uncertainty along with the burden of grief. Instead of drowning herself in sorrow, Louisa penned these words:

'Tis so sweet to trust in Jesus,
Just to take Him at His Word,
Just to rest upon His promise,
Just to know, "Thus saith the Lord."

CHORUS:

Jesus, Jesus, how I trust Him!

How I've proved Him o'er and o'er!

Jesus, Jesus, precious Jesus!

O for grace to trust Him more.

Indeed, nothing could be sweeter in life than to trust in Jesus. I've never experienced the loss of a husband, and consequently, my livelihood, but every day presents its own challenges. That's true for anyone. We all have things happen to us—good and bad—that give us the opportunity to trust.

My brother will be interviewing for job a next week. Many questions arise out of that one situation, many changes for our family. My sister-in-law and I were just discussing how hard it is to wait, not knowing what the outcome will be. "And yet," she said, "what choice do we have? Worry or trust. I'm choosing to take it one day at a time and trust in Jesus."

Trust really is at the heart of peace. When we allow ourselves to be consumed by fear, stress, or anxiety, we have no peace. That's because we're not trusting. It's very difficult sometimes, but even in this we are not to rely on ourselves. God gives us the grace we need to trust in Jesus. I find that if I take one step toward Him in trust, even just a prayer that expresses my weak desire to trust Him, He meets that desire with grace, and gives me the strength to trust Him more.

No matter what comes, we can rest on God's promises. Louisa Stead trusted them enough to transform her tragedy into a beautiful hymn for the ages. We can take Him at His word. He is trustworthy—and life is sweet when we put our trust in Him.

> *Jesus, life is sweet when my heart is trusting in You. I want trusting to be my way of life. Help me trust You in simplicity—just to take You at Your word and rest on Your promises, knowing You are in control and You know best.*

Stormy Weather

By now it was dark, and Jesus had not yet joined them.

A strong wind was blowing and the waters grew rough....

They saw Jesus approaching the boat, walking on the water;

and they were terrified. But he said to them, "It is I; don't be afraid."

JOHN 6:17–20 NIV

This past week has brought some of the worst weather to northwest Arkansas that I can remember. We've had torrential rain, flooding, and golf ball-sized hail. In some places, there have even been tornadoes.

Just the other night my family was sitting down to dinner when a friend called (she knew we wouldn't have the TV on). "There is a tornado warning in effect for Franklin County. You need to turn on the radio and get in your safest place."

So, we gathered up our plates and went to the kids' bathroom, the only room in our house that doesn't have a window.

Huddled together on little stools, we finished our dinner, read from the Bible, prayed, and sang songs. Dot, our Boston Terrier, took turns lounging across our laps.

When we emerged, we found the outside world stripped bare, new. There were branches littered around our deck. Rivulets of water ran through our yard. The atmosphere seemed to hold its breath with an eerie calm, and there was the shadow of a giant, black cloud. Beyond the clouds, however, was a brilliant sunset. And suspended for miles across the sky was a spectacular double rainbow. It was as if God was assuring the world that He was still in charge.

The ethereal beauty of the rainbows following such chaos refreshed all of our spirits. I usually think more about how He is with us in the midst of the storm, and indeed He is. However, it was nice to be reminded that He is on the throne through it all, and that bad weather always passes.

There are two accounts of Jesus walking on water when His disciples were caught in storms, and one in which He rises from sleep on their boat and commands the tempest to be still. Clearly, storms don't bother Jesus, or make Him nervous in the least. They serve His will just as much as the rainbows.

When storms come in our lives—and they inevitably will—all we need to remember is that He is with us. He has things covered; we need not worry. Sure, we need to take proper precautions as good stewards of the lives He's given us. But ultimately, He is in control. He works things together for our good. No storm lasts forever, and He brings newness and beauty out of chaos.

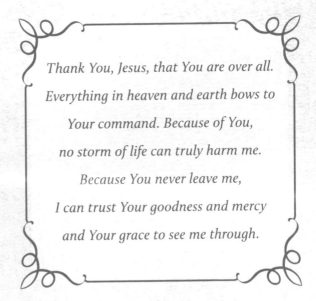

Thank You, Jesus, that You are over all.
Everything in heaven and earth bows to
Your command. Because of You,
no storm of life can truly harm me.
Because You never leave me,
I can trust Your goodness and mercy
and Your grace to see me through.

The Invincible Man

He took Peter and the two sons of Zebedee along with him,

and he began to be sorrowful and troubled.

MATTHEW 26:37 NIV

This scene in the Garden of Gethsemane has always fascinated me. I believe it was the most vulnerable moment of Jesus' life. In Matthew 26:38, He pleads with His friends, *Stay with me while I pray. My soul is overwhelmed with sorrow to the point of death.*

Notwithstanding this scene, I rarely think of Jesus as needy. He was, after all, the invincible man. Look how He demonstrated His power when He was tempted by Satan in the desert. Forty days and nights, and He did not succumb.

Throughout His ministry of preaching, teaching, healing, etc., there's also certain aloofness I sense in Him. It's not that He doesn't love people, because of course He does. I adore how He embraced little children, and showed His compassion to the poor and the sick. What I'm talking about is those times he withdraws "to a quiet place," or falls asleep when everyone else on the boat is awake, or when He writes in the dirt while people are questioning Him about what to do with the woman caught in sin.

There are things we can learn from this aloofness, among them the ability to separate ourselves from the fray. To remain calm in the midst of drama. Especially when we are in a stressful situation.

Here, in the Garden of Gethsemane, though, we see such a tender side of Jesus as He exposes His need to His friends. *Stay with me. My soul is overwhelmed.*

Words like that are hard for me to say—to anyone. I have a wonderful, supportive husband and extended family, and a host of friends. But I don't like to be in a vulnerable position with anyone. Not really.

As Christians we sometimes think we are always supposed to be strong, always the givers and never the takers. And that is partially true. I'd certainly rather lean toward the side of strength and giving than neediness, just as Jesus did. But when a need is real, we need to be able to admit it. To ask those who love us for help. To receive what they have to offer by way of comfort.

That is one of the sub-tragedies of the scene in Gethsemane—Jesus' friends didn't come through. They *fell asleep.* He's in there fighting the battle of His life (not to mention the universal consequences!) and they can't stay awake with Him. They didn't find it important enough to lose sleep over.

I know they were only human like we are, and we can't always be there for everyone. Sometimes we're going to let down the people who matter the most. But when someone we love is obviously needy and overwhelmed, Jesus wants us to respond with open hearts and hands. And when that needy one is ourself, we need to have the humility to let others know.

Jesus, I'd like to think that if I'd been in the garden with You I wouldn't have fallen asleep. But without Your grace I can't get past my selfishness, my own physical and spiritual neediness, to minister to the needs of others. Give me Your heart, Lord, to be humble enough to ask for help when I need it, and to be humble enough to give my help to others when You ordain it.

Lucky

This I call to mind and therefore I have hope: Because of the Lord's
great love we are not consumed, for his compassions never fail.
They are new every morning; great is your faithfulness.

LAMENTATIONS 3:21–23 NIV

I've got a little bulldog who sits by me when I write at
my parents' house. Actually, he's not sitting right now.
He's lying down—sprawled out beside me in their oversized
chair. Snoring.

This dog can't hear, and he only has one eye that works.
When he barks, he sounds like a cross between a coyote and a
squealing pig. He also has a crooked leg and a bit of a limp from
being run over by a car. When we got him several years ago he
was a total charity case—and my mother was what some would
call a "sucker."

My dad named him "Lucky." My mom disagreed with this

name. She said they were the lucky ones, to get such a good dog for free. But after seeing her extra special care for the dog and all of his, shall we say, "special" needs for all of these years, the name has stuck. We all call him Lucky. And lucky he is.

Abandoned by his previous owners, Lucky used to be frightened almost to death to be alone. You could see it in his eye. If my mom went to the store and dad wasn't in the house, he nearly scratched a hole in the door of their laundry room till someone returned to let him out. He also used to go crazy whenever people would come over. It was like new people made him a nervous wreck, and excited him all at once. He caused quite a scene.

But that was the old Lucky. The new Lucky still has issues, but he's mostly a lap dog. I guess he's been loved long enough now that he can relax and enjoy life.

Lucky reminds me of me. There's nothing inherently pleasing about me that would make Jesus pick me for a companion. I'm more of a charity case. I've got plenty of blind spots, and often don't listen well to commands. I can't always communicate well. People make me nervous as well as excited, and I often botch things up. I'm not especially obedient. I get scared and doubtful when I can't immediately see Jesus, as though, like so many others have, He would desert our friendship, leaving me to fend for myself.

And yet He has brought me into His kingdom and called me His friend. I sit in a place of honor. He washes me and feeds me and tends to all of my needs. He speaks to my heart, deeper things than what I can hear with my ears. He reveals Himself in ways I've never seen before. And most of all, He stays with me. He won't ever leave me or forsake me. I'm not too much trouble for Him.

Perhaps one day I'll be loved long enough that I can just rest myself in the Lord. Maybe one day soon. Like Lucky, I want to enjoy the life that He's given me, and enjoy Him—in all of His mercy, His goodness, and His love.

Jesus, thank You for loving me so much.
I know I could never do anything to
earn it—or to lose it, for that matter.
What wondrous love is this?
I want to rest in Your arms—
sprawl out in Your presence
and provision today and every day.

Hope Blooms

We have peace with God through our Lord Jesus Christ,

through whom also we have access by faith into this grace

in which we stand, and rejoice in hope of the glory of God....

Hope does not disappoint.

ROMANS 5:1–2, 5 NKJV

Not long ago, I was asked to speak at the funeral of a friend. It was one of the biggest honors of my life, and also one of the hardest things I have ever done. My friend was forty-two, had never hurt a flea, and had left behind a husband, two children, and a loving extended family. She lost her life when a tornado touched down in the tiny community of Etna, Arkansas.

What can we say at a time like this? Dealing with my own grief, I felt anger rise when anyone dared to suggest it was God's will, or offered one of any other numerous trite statements people say to sum up an incomprehensible reality. Words dropped like rain and made rivulets in my brain that all eventually spilled into a sea of nothingness. And yet, it was my job to say something. I asked God to give me courage. To help me be honest and faithful. To use me, if He would, to bring comfort.

In the few days leading up to the funeral, I spent a lot of time with my head down, looking at the ground. One morning I observed the beginning of a process that helped me gain perspective. First, I noticed just the tip of a single green blade. It shot up through the ground like a sword, as if some unseen hand was clasping it, declaring from below the surface, *I am not conquered. I am alive.* The next thing I saw was another blade, and another, and then they each began to unfold. Soon the bloom of an exotically beautiful white calla lily graced the edge of my sidewalk. Shaped like a trumpet, it heralded hope.

I decided that was what I most wanted to do at the funeral. Offer hope.

When I stood at the podium with my knees shaking, I looked out at the broken faces of those who had loved and lost so much. I was able to tell a few stories about my friend and celebrate how her beauty graced our lives. But in the end, what comforted me, and I believe the people listening, is the hope we have in Jesus.

The honest truth is that being a Christian doesn't mean

we sugarcoat tragedy, or form clichés for things we don't understand. The whole message of Jesus is that we stare suffering straight in the face—we acknowledge it in all of its ugliness—and yet we have hope. We cry out with Job, "Though He slay me, yet will I trust Him" (Job 13:15 KJV). We dare to believe that death is not the end of our story. And we know, because He promises, He is with us through it all. Jesus is near.

Paul writes in Romans 8:35-39, "Who will separate us from the love of Christ? Will tribulation, or distress, or persecution, or famine, or nakedness, or peril, or sword?... In all these things we overwhelmingly conquer through Him who loved us. [Nothing] will be able to separate us from the love of God, which is in Christ Jesus our Lord" (NASB).

Thank You, Jesus, that I can place my hope in You, even in the midst of life's greatest losses. Help me to know, no matter what happens, that You are near. I cling to You.

High Places

The LORD God is my strength, and he will make my feet
like hinds' feet, and he will make me to walk upon mine high places.

HABAKUK 3:19 KJV

When Stone and I got ready to build a house, my parents told us we could pick out any place on their ranch that we wanted. Since the ranch backs up to the Arkansas River, we hiked and rode four-wheelers all along the northwest border, looking for the perfect view.

A few years before, we'd been through a low time in our marriage. Thankful for how God brought us through, we knew this home would be something really special—the place we planned to stay, where we would raise our family together. We prayed that the Lord would lead us to where He wanted us to build.

Some of the ranch has rolling hills that lead down to the river. The view is pretty, and you could set your house right in the woods, with the river down below. One place we looked at had a nice pond beside it and lovely trees and pasture in the front. We thought about that place long and hard.

But then we rode up to the high places. There's a crescent-shaped section of bluff almost at the far end of the property. My brother's house sits out on one point, like a sentinel on the edge of the world. Starting there, we followed the bluff line to where my parents' land ends.

Tromping through the woods, about midway across the crescent, my eyes were drawn to something. Strangely, a cactus was there, in the middle of the trees, and it was blooming. I stooped to study it and noted how sharp were its thorns—they looked lethal—and yet how lovely and delicate the yellow flower that bloomed within their shelter. We walked on. Hugging the edge of the forest was a sheer cliff that plunged five hundred feet down to the river. In one spot, however, a moss-covered rock jutted out from the cliff like a table. And right in its point we spotted a cedar tree, shaped like a bonsai, against all odds growing up out of the rock.

"I believe this is it," I told Stone. "The Lord has brought us to this place." He agreed, and now our house overlooks that spot.

There's a beautiful old book by Hannah Hurnard called *Hinds' Feet on High Places*. It's an allegory in which a crippled deer named Much Afraid learns to walk on the high places with her Shepherd. She encounters many obstacles throughout her journey, but she has two veiled companions who help her develop strength. Their names are Sorrow and Suffering. By the time her feet become strong enough for the high places, her name has changed to Acceptance with Joy.

Much Afraid doesn't realize what a gift Sorrow and Suffering are until she notices how strong her feet have become. It can be the same with us. Sometimes all we can see are the thorns and the rocks. But if we are patient, and keep moving forward with the Lord at His pace, under His direction, He'll take us to the high places. The flower will bloom. The tree will take root and burst forth out of the rock, declaring the glory of His name. And homes will be built on that foundation. Sorrow may last for a while. But for children of the King, joy comes in the morning.

Jesus, You are my hope. Thank You that You lead me out of sorrow and into Your joy. Take my hand. I will follow You, Shepherd, wherever You lead.

Jesus Freaks

For I am not ashamed of the gospel of Christ,
for it is the power of God to salvation for everyone who believes.

ROMANS 1:16 NKJV

I have a distant cousin named David. I'd only met him once, when I was little, until this year when he came to Arkansas from Oregon for a visit. After about fifteen minutes of conversation, I could already tell: David was a Jesus Freak.

You know the type. You can be talking about anything—the weather, a ballgame, a book you've read—and somehow the conversation always gets back to Jesus. It's like there's nothing else that interests them. It's "Jesus this and Jesus that" ad infinitum. Sometimes all of that Jesus talk makes "normal" people uncomfortable. *Enough about Jesus already*, we're thinking. But David never gets enough.

I suppose he has his reasons. He's not really a normal

person. He's had three near-death experiences that I know of, and there could be possibly more. First, as a career firefighter, he had a terrible accident that nearly killed him. That was many years ago. Then he got cancer—severe cancer—but David survived that too. His latest brush with death, which occurred since his visit to Arkansas, was blood poisoning.

The world—even the Christian world—scratches its head when encountering a David. We don't know what to do with these people. What do you say to someone like that?

My friend Sandy Terry is the same way. According to doctors, she should be dead right now. Five years ago she was in stage four breast cancer. Today, she's cancer-free. Though she does have to live with damage from chemo, she doesn't let it rob her of purpose. In fact, I've rarely seen her down.

Sandy and I met for coffee the other day and ended up talking about her favorite subject, which, like my cousin David, is Jesus. I asked her to shed light for me on a perspective that never seems to waver. Her Jesus obsession, if you will.

She laughed. And then she told me very frankly that she just didn't have time for anything else. What cancer had done for her was to simplify everything. "What you realize when you're close to death," she said with her blue eyes dancing, "is that nothing else matters in life. Literally nothing. Only Jesus."

In that moment the hairs on the back of my neck stood

on end. What Sandy said made a lot of sense, and for one tiny split second God drew back the veil of my human experience. I felt like I was able to see the world and my place in it through her—and David's—eyes. What I saw held such splendor it was almost enough to make me jealous, just for that blink of time. But not quite. Because I saw what their suffering had produced in them. True intimacy. Identification with the cross. Focus. And an immediate sense of eternity, far stronger and more real than what we normal people can see. It kind of makes you want to be a Jesus Freak.

> *Oh, Jesus. That I would not have to be taken to the raw edge of my human frailty to be able to behold Your beauty, and be consumed by it. Thank You for broken vessels—these Jesus Freaks—that You have refined like gold. What a powerful message You've entrusted to them. May we have ears to listen, hearts to receive. For they speak the truth with authority of what really matters to all of us. Help me be a Jesus Freak.*

A Deeper Hunger

God hath chosen the foolish things of the world
to confound the wise; and God hath chosen the weak things
of the world to confound the things which are mighty.

1 Corinthians 1:27 kjv

The other morning there was an interview on NPR with the Hitchens brothers that caught by attention. I knew about Christopher Hitchens, the world-renowned British atheist, but I didn't know he had a brother named Peter who is a Christian. They both stated their positions in the interview, and the conflict that has ensued as a result of their differing views. Apparently Peter, who is as distinguished as Christopher, if not as outspoken, has been arguing in favor of Christianity with his atheist brother for years. With Christopher's diagnosis of terminal cancer, they have called a cease-fire. Peter said, in essence, "I don't want to argue anymore. I just want to love him in the time we have left."

When I heard that, I prayed that his love would win his brother over—before it's too late.

Listening to Peter Hitchens explain his conversion experience—out of intellectual pride, essentially, into the light of Biblical truth—I was reminded of a poem by Whittier, called "Worth Treasuring":

> We search the world for truth; we cull
> The good, the pure, the beautiful,
> From graven stone and written scroll,
> From all old flower fields of the soul;
> And weary seekers of the best,
> We come back laden from our quest,
> To find that all the sages said
> Is in the book our mothers read.

I'm a peon compared to either one of the Hitchens brothers, but I experience this kind of conversion on a regular basis. As an academic and a seeker of truth, I read a lot of stuff. I listen to a lot of smart people. I get enamored by the words of gifted writers and intellectuals, lose myself in beautiful music, and I love to look at good art. These kinds of things feed my soul.

But as saturated as my soul becomes, there's a deeper hunger nothing in this world can fill. Harper was singing about it this morning, in preparation for his "special music" at church:

"I want You more than gold or silver, only You can satisfy. You alone are the real joy-giver and the apple of my eye" (Martin Nystrom).

We talked about what those words meant. For every individual there are different things we seek to fill our hunger. For me it might be stimulating conversation, a new book deal, a grand piano. For a child it's a win in baseball, a good grades bonus, a new toy. All of those things are nice. But for every individual there's only one thing—one person—who can satisfy the deepest longings of the spirit. That one person is Jesus. And He's free and available to all.

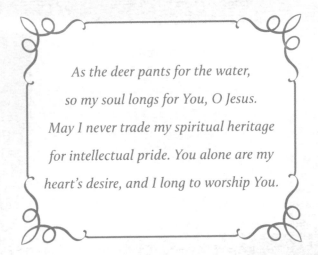

As the deer pants for the water,

so my soul longs for You, O Jesus.

May I never trade my spiritual heritage

for intellectual pride. You alone are my

heart's desire, and I long to worship You.

Falling

The eternal God is your refuge,
and underneath are the everlasting arms.

DEUTERONOMY 33:27 NIV

Somebody said, "All truth is God's truth" and I believe it. Otherwise how could a movie about an alcoholic country singer who nearly wrecks a child's life minister God's truth to me? Don't laugh. It happened.

When I'm writing something long and taxing, my brain works so hard it feels like it's turning into a lump of mush. To try to keep that from happening, I take breaks in spurts and think about something totally unrelated to what I'm working on. For example, as I've written this book I've read a series of novels set in ancient Rome. Every time I start feeling a little nutty, I just jump into the world of the gladiators for a little while. Pretty soon the devotional side of my brain is rested and ready to write again. It really does work wonders.

One of my recent escapes was the movie *Crazy Heart*. It not only provided a break from my work, it also got me thinking. It contains this nugget in the lyrics of one of its songs:

It's funny how falling feels like flying for a little while.

That could have come straight out of Proverbs. In fact, it practically does. Proverbs 16:18 says, "Pride goes before destruction, a haughty spirit before a fall" (NIV).

I can so relate to these parallel sentiments. It never fails. Every single time I'm flying high on self, I think I've got something down, I've arrived, it's in the bag—wham. I start to fall. Every. Time. You'd think I'd learn. And I *am* trying. The Bible says God disciplines the ones He loves. I'm trying to learn my lessons, because I like getting spanked about as much as my kids do.

Regardless of what happens in *Crazy Heart*, falling, for the Christian, seems to involve a series of steps. The first is when, in our pride, we actually think we're flying. Then, like Icarus, the wax on those wings melts in the light of the Son. We begin to fall. During the actual falling—that space of time that we are out of control and can do nothing about it—we become terrified. It's a scary moment when we realize we could fall to our doom. The cool thing about Jesus, though, is that when we cry out to Him, He's there to break our fall. Like the Bible says, "underneath are the everlasting arms." He catches us, and we realize His arms are where we're meant to be...where we are safe even from ourselves...where we want to stay for all eternity.

Jesus, I thank You that You're always there to pick me up when I fall. Help me rest in Your embrace today and keep me humble in my spirit, that I may be gentler, meeker, quietly stronger. More like You.

Birthday Money

Each of you should give what you have decided in your heart to give,

not reluctantly or under compulsion, for God loves a cheerful giver.

2 CORINTHIANS 9:7 NIV

As so often happens, a principle of the kingdom of heaven was illustrated to me by a means one might least expect. Giving—how God sees it, and therefore what it really means—has been taught to me not by any Bible scholar, nor the person who gives the most to church or charity, not through the experience of receiving a lavish gift, but by a little child. My eight-year-old son, Harper.

Harper's birthday is in October. He thought he wanted a kayak for his present, so instead of gifts, everyone in the family gave him money to go toward the kayak's purchase. However, after shopping for kayaks, he decided that wasn't what he wanted after all. (I was more than a little relieved.) That evening, we laid out his pile of money on his bed. I suggested several things he might do with it.

"You need a new guitar."

"I'd like a new bike."

"How about some winter clothes?"

"There's a fishing pole I've been wanting, and a new gun."

I started to write this all down so he could make a little budget.

"Wait, Mom." He counted the bills. "I want to set this much aside for Christmas."

The amount was a lot. I didn't know what he was doing.

"You won't need that for Christmas, baby. That money's for your birthday. Everybody will still buy you presents for Christmas."

"I know." He smiled at me. "It's not for me. It's so I can buy everybody else presents."

He had counted out several dollars each to spend on everyone in the family.

I tried to argue with him. "That's really sweet, honey, but you don't need to do that. Maybe set aside a few dollars, but not that much. You need to spend your birthday money on you."

"No, Mom." He put the money into a pouch and placed it in a drawer. "I've made up my mind. This is what I want to do."

Sure enough, come Christmas morning, there were presents under the tree for everybody—from Harper. He presented each one with a flourish. Adelaide received a bow and arrow, along with some caps for her gun. Stone opened a nice grooming kit. Grace received a game she wanted, and I got a new sweat suit. The look on Harper's face as we opened each one is something I hope to remember always. It was joy. Rapture. Pure delight. He took pleasure in the presents he received, but the experience of giving far surpassed it.

Acts 20:35 says, "It is more blessed to give than to receive" (KJV). I want the Lord to see that look on my face—the same look as Harper's—the next time I give something to Him. No compulsion, not holding back, just an outflow of my love and honor. No motive, other than a desire to see Him smile. What joy would fill His heart. What joy would fill mine! If being Harper's mother is any measure of how God loves, I now understand what it means to "love a cheerful giver."

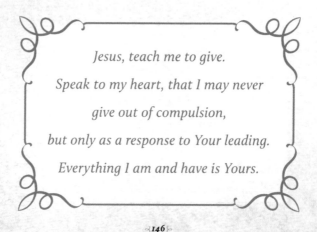

Jesus, teach me to give.
Speak to my heart, that I may never
give out of compulsion,
but only as a response to Your leading.
Everything I am and have is Yours.

Lent

Just as Christ was raised from the dead through the glory of the Father,
we too may live a new life.

ROMANS 6:4 NIV

I've never celebrated "High Church" traditions but I have a lot of friends who do. Some celebrate Fat Tuesday with gusto and then on Ash Wednesday move directly into Lent, a season many associate with penance. With my background, Fat Tuesday I can handle, but Lent itself has never held much appeal for me.

This year on Ash Wednesday I received by way of Facebook a link to The Huffington Post. There was an article there by Sister Joan Chittister, who challenged me to think about Lent in a new way. She wrote: "If penance is all that Lent is about...it makes the spiritual life some kind of arithmetical balancing act. I do so many penances for so much human misadventure...the important thing is that I remember to come out even. But Lent is a much greater moment in life than that."

Finally, she gives the most beautiful description of Lent I have ever read: "Lent is a call to weep for what we could have been and are not. Lent is the grace to grieve for what we should have done and did not. Lent is the opportunity to change what we ought to change but have not. Lent is not about penance. Lent is about becoming, doing, and changing whatever it is that is blocking the fullness of life in us right now. Lent is a summons to live anew."

I'm not trying to push Lent on anybody. At least not in any traditional, religious sense. But what I am advocating is the sister's "summons to live anew." Look at the language she uses. *Becoming, doing, and changing whatever it is that is blocking the fullness of life in us right now.* In other words, let's get rid of everything that hinders the Spirit of Jesus. If that's what Lent is, well, we should all continually celebrate the season. Sign me up!

Jesus, thank You that the Christian life is not a life of penance. It's not a balancing act between the good things I do and the bad. You died on the cross to give us fullness of life. I'm rending my heart before You now because I've failed in embracing that life. I don't always respond appropriately to who You are and what You've done. I'm truly sorry. I desire to renew my commitment to You. Transform me now by Your love that I might be the person I was meant to be in You.

The Perfect Gift

And God is able to make all grace abound toward you;
that ye, always having all sufficiency in all things, may abound to
every good work.... Thanks be unto God for his unspeakable gift.

2 CORINTHIANS 9:8,15 KJV

There's an old saying, "You can give without loving, but you can't love without giving." I find that to be so true. I've been guilty at times of giving out of obligation rather than love, but for those I truly love, it's like I just can't give enough. I see things every time I'm shopping that I want to buy for my kids. My mom and sister-in-law too. It can be as simple as a nail polish color I think they'd like, or as expensive as a new swimming pool. My heart longs for them to have things they enjoy, because I love them so much. Love brings out generosity, and if my budget allowed, my family and friends would have every material thing their hearts desire.

Jesus, the lover of our souls, was God's greatest gift to humankind. He was also a giver. Just think of the cross. But I've found something interesting in studying the life of Jesus—He doesn't seem too big on giving material gifts.

Since He was God and could do whatever He wanted, He could have made coins appear, or fine linen, or fishing boats, or whatever was cool back then. He could have showered His followers with gifts. But He didn't. Throughout the gospels we see Him providing for their basic needs, like food and shelter, and...that's it. There's not ever a single account of Him giving someone a new pair of sandals. It's kind of weird in my way of thinking.

I believe He refrained from giving his loved ones a lot of material gifts because He had something so much better to give them: Himself. Paul writes in Colossians, "You have everything when you have Christ." When Jesus gave Himself away, He gave everything His followers could possibly need. They needed forgiveness. They needed understanding. They needed compassion, grace, leadership, love. Everything the world needed then and needs now comes in one package. Jesus.

Since Jesus lives His life in us, we too can give Him away. I've found that my kids want my presence more than they want toys, and my mother would rather have me visit than to receive a new blouse. They need to see the character of Jesus in me. What more could I ever give anyone than the compassion of Christ? The patience and understanding of Jesus? The grace and love of a Savior? Material gifts are great, and there's a place for them in our lives. But if we really want to give the good stuff, we'll give people more and more of Him.

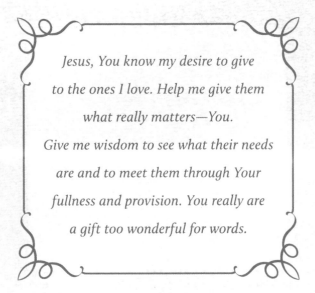

Jesus, You know my desire to give to the ones I love. Help me give them what really matters—You.
Give me wisdom to see what their needs are and to meet them through Your fullness and provision. You really are a gift too wonderful for words.

The Pursuit of Happiness

For whosoever wants to save their life will lose it,

but whoever loses their life for me will find it.

MATTHEW 16:25 NIV

I've often thought about the pursuit of happiness. It's in our Declaration of Independence, and either as a cause or effect, it seems to be the "American Dream." But it seems ironic that so many people who attain the "American Dream" are unhappy, while happiness comes to others in the unlikeliest of places.

Take celebrities, for example. A few of them are able to carve out what appears to be a happy life. The vast majority, however, seem absolutely miserable. Every time we turn around, some rich, famous person is in trouble with the law, or going to drug rehab, or worse.

I was personal friends during my college years with a

family that was uber-successful in the banking business. They seemed to have it all: beauty, wealth, a glamorous life. Sadly, the parents are now divorced and every one of the kids has also suffered a failed marriage. I know they would say, because they've said it to me before, that they would rather be happy than have such a high social status. Their financial success has also been their downfall, and now—so sadly—they are picking up the pieces of a shattered life.

Compare these stories with the story of Gail Hillard, who lies in a bed all day because of a degenerative bone disease in her back. She's my former piano teacher, and every December I take my kids caroling at her house at Christmas. Every year we think we're going to cheer her up, but instead she brings us joy with her wonderful attitude. One time I asked her how she stands it, lying there all of the time.

"The Lord is with me," she chuckled. "We get along quite well."

She never lets us leave without letting her know how to pray for us. From the confines of her bed, she's an intercessory prayer warrior.

Then there is my friend in Sunday school class who deals with so many issues at once I can't keep up with all of her prayer needs. Her ex-husband is constantly causing problems for her and her kids; one of her children has serious health problems that induce regular stress; she works and goes to college, and manages to get to Sunday school with a smile on her face and a sparkle in her eye. She is a barrel of fun. It's clear that in spite of her circumstances, she is happy.

I believe the reason for our happiness lies in our relationship with Jesus—in losing ourselves in His love. Though Gail and my Sunday school friend may have a "right" to be unhappy because of their circumstances, they have taken a higher road. The calling of Christ leads us onward and upward out of self and into a life of trust, and service to others.

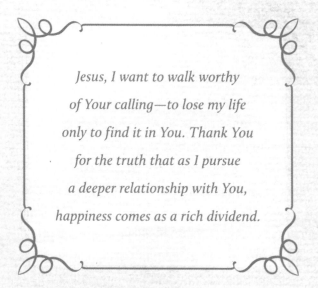

Jesus, I want to walk worthy of Your calling—to lose my life only to find it in You. Thank You for the truth that as I pursue a deeper relationship with You, happiness comes as a rich dividend.

The Scarlet Cord

She tied the scarlet cord in the window.

Joshua 2:21 NIV

I like to look for epiphanies—appearances of Jesus, or symbols of Him—in the Old Testament. One of my favorites is found in the story of Rahab, the prostitute who lived in Jericho. The book of Joshua records how she hid the Israelite spies when they sneaked inside the walls to survey the city. One of her great lines is in Joshua 2:11, when she says, "The Lord your God is God in heaven above and on earth below" (NIV).

This confession of her faith leads to the salvation of her whole family. The spies give her a scarlet cord to hang in her window. They tell her that when the Israelite army marches through the city, her house will be spared, and everyone in it, because of the scarlet cord.

The color scarlet is significant. I believe it symbolizes

Jesus' blood. Just like the blood of the lamb that was applied to doorposts at Passover, the scarlet cord protected Rahab and her family from death. Everyone else in Jericho was destroyed. But Rahab the prostitute was saved.

Something else that is very cool about this story is that in Matthew 1, when the writer gives the genealogy of Jesus, Rahab is one of the only women who are listed. It's mostly dads, with the exception of Tamar, and then in verse five we come to Boaz, *whose mother was Rahab*. Of course Boaz "begot" Obed; Obed, Jesse; and Jesse, David (as in King David); and so on and so forth...till we get to Joseph, Mary, and Jesus the Christ.

I'm glad we get to find out the rest of Rahab's story. There's a lot of hope in it. She went from wearing the title of prostitute, like a scarlet letter, to being saved by a scarlet cord. A symbol of Jesus' blood brought her salvation, and as a consequence, her blood ran through Jesus' veins. That's Rahab's legacy. She's the great-great-great-great (etc.) grandma of Jesus!

What's your story? Is there an epiphany in it—an appearance of Jesus? What about lately? Maybe you know Him but it's been awhile since You sensed He was near. Does something hold you back from drawing too close? We all wear the labels of things we're not proud of, whether they're visible or on our hearts.

No matter who you are, or where you've been, Jesus offers hope. God could have chosen anyone in Jericho to help the spies, but He chose a prostitute named Rahab. And the last time we see her, she's not called "prostitute" anymore. She's called the grandmother of the King of Kings.

Jesus, You're just awesome.

The Bible, and the way Your scarlet

thread is woven through the tapestry

of human history, is simply amazing.

Breathtaking in its genius. You command

my worship and praise. Thank You for

choosing people like Rahab—people with

no spiritual credentials—to participate

in the miracle of Your salvation.

And I thank You for choosing me.

You are my one and only hope—give me

eyes to see glimpses of Your scarlet thread

in my life today, and every day.

Thy Will Be Done

He fell with his face to the ground and prayed,
"My Father, if it is possible, may this cup be taken from me.
Yet not as I will, but as you will."

MATTHEW 26:39 NIV

Jesus' prayer in the Garden of Gethsemane is amazing, for so many reasons. One is just that it's so impossible. He was God. Creator, Ruler, Sustainer. And yet there He is, with His face pressed to the ground, crying out to the heavens for mercy.

When we view Him through the lens of His humanity, though, it's almost just as amazing. For what human, facing torture and death on a cross, would be able to submit to that fate as the will of God? Only a hero. Only one totally focused on His mission. And only one who truly trusted in the sovereignty and goodness of His God.

Jesus' prayer is an example to every believer of how we should respond under pressure. Whether our task is emotional, physical, or spiritual, the biggest difficulty lies in our acceptance of it as coming to us from the hand of a loving God. His sovereignty makes this true, but it doesn't make it easy.

I think that's why I love it that Jesus wrestles with His destiny. He doesn't just swallow what's in the cup without questioning its contents. He begs His Father to take it from Him. He pleads. He cries. He sweats blood. And in the end, He submits. By the time Judas gets there with the soldiers, He's ready to drink it down.

Jesus' example is empowering to me. Because of His prayer in Gethsemane I don't assume that everything I pray for is God's will. I figure, if *Jesus* in all of His humanity had desires that were contrary to God's will—like His own physical survival—then surely I will too. Every person I want to be healed may not be healed. Every thorn may not be removed from my flesh. Every cup may not be taken from me. Why or why not? I have no idea. Because only God knows best.

We may wrestle with the direction God is taking us, the decisions we have to make, how to deal with the people we would rather not deal with. But when it is all said and done, most of us want to do what God leads us to do. It's our deepest desire, our deepest craving as His followers. In the end, the cross triumphs over self.

That's the ultimate theme of Gethsemane: *If it's possible for You to give me what I want, I want it. Badly. But if not, well, I want Your will more.*

Jesus, You have given us such a beautiful example of total and complete trust in the Lord. I pray today that You will use the trials of my life for Your glory— to make me more like You, especially in this area of trust. I want to love and submit to God with all of my heart, soul, mind, and strength. Thank You for empowering me to accept and follow His will, no matter what He asks.

Touching Jesus

She had suffered a great deal.... When she heard about Jesus,
she came up behind him in the crowd and touched his cloak,
because she thought, "If I touch his clothes, I will be healed."

The woman described in the above verses had been bleeding for twelve years. She'd been to doctors who couldn't help her, and all the time her condition kept growing worse. Can you imagine?

The fact is, many of us can. Scores of people suffer with health issues every day. Others suffer from grief, poverty, and injustice. Still others deal with the stress of an unhealthy relationship, or the pain of past abuse. The list of possibilities is endless. Like this lady, we may struggle on and on for years with little hope of relief.

But the Bible says that when she heard about Jesus...she

thought, *He could help me.* So she chased Him down! Worked herself through the crowd and any other obstacles and touched the hem of His garment. And instantly—she was healed.

I believe Jesus cares about us just like He cared about this woman. I believe He is interested in our problems, just as He was interested in hers. There's nothing too big, too small, too gross or insignificant that He won't help us with it. Like in the case of this woman, He is ready to give us the power we need to be made whole.

All of Jesus' gifts are gifts of grace, but sometimes it takes determination to access them. Look closely at the lady in Mark 5. She sought after Jesus with her whole heart. May have made a fool of herself running after Him. But at some point it didn't matter to her what she had to do—she was determined to catch hold of Him. And when she did, He met her need.

He will meet yours and mine too.

Jeremiah 29:13 says, "You will seek Me and find Me, when you seek Me with all of your heart" (NIV). Sometimes the answer isn't instant, like it was for this woman. However, the Bible does say she had suffered for twelve years. Maybe she'd been seeking that whole time—she probably had, we know she'd been to doctors. But this was her moment. The moment Jesus was near enough to touch. What would we ask Him to heal? to change? to help us overcome?

We're not given the terms of His timing, but we are given

His terms for seeking. He wants us to seek Him with all of our hearts. When we do, He promises we'll find Him. Like the woman in the story, we'll touch Him. And He will make us whole.

Dear Jesus, how I need a touch from You today. Send Your power and heal me in this area of my life:_____

_____

_____. I know You are the One who can change my situation, or, if You desire, to change me in it.

A Wee Little Man

Now behold, there was a man named Zacchaeus who was a chief

tax collector, and he was rich. And he sought to see who Jesus was,

but could not because of the crowd, for he was of short stature.

So he ran ahead and climbed up into a sycamore tree to see Him,

for He was going to pass that way. And when Jesus came to the place,

He looked up and saw him, and said to him, "Zacchaeus,

make haste and come down, for today I must stay at your house."

So he made haste and came down, and received Him joyfully.

LUKE 19:2–6 NKJV

As a child in Sunday school I loved to sing the little song about Zacchaeus: *Zacchaeus was a wee little man, and a wee little man was he....*

I always thought it was funny, the idea of a grown man climbing a tree, but even then it was impressed upon me how much Zacchaeus wanted to see Jesus. I've always thought it was pure curiosity that drew him. And it may have been. But as I look at the story with fresh eyes, it seems there might have been something more.

Could it be that the Bible tells us Zacchaeus' background so that we are able to discern his need? He was a chief tax collector, basically an outcast, even though he was rich. That description seems loaded: materially anchored, emotionally bereft. A sell-out. Poor little rich guy with no friends.

Then the Bible says that *when Jesus came to the place, He looked up and saw him.* When He came to the place. That seems to suggest that Jesus was walking along and the Spirit moved Him—He felt directed—to look up in a certain place. And there was Zacchaeus. Jesus *looked up and saw him.*

I wish I could have been a bird on a branch near Zacchaeus. I can only imagine the look in Jesus' eyes when He *saw him.* It seems to me that Luke, in this passage, uses a doctor's precision to set the scene. Was this the first time someone saw Zacchaeus? Saw into his heart and soul? Certainly, no one had looked at him with eyes like Jesus.

And then the best part: Jesus came to stay with him. It didn't matter what Zacchaeus had done. Who he was on the outside did not impress Jesus, and who he was on the inside did not make Jesus turn away. Zacchaeus "sought to see Him" and in the bargain, Zacchaeus was seen, accepted, befriended, loved.

Perhaps for the very first time.

Do you ever feel "unseen"? I do. Sometimes I do some pretty strange things to get attention. But isn't it worth it to be considered strange, goofy, or freaky if Jesus looks you right in the eye and sees you? Really sees you? I'd climb a tree for that.

> *Jesus, thank You that You see me where I am at this very moment. You see everything I've been, everything I am, and everything I want to be. Thank You for taking the time to stop and draw near to me. Stay with me always. Like Zacchaeus, I receive You joyfully.*

Jesus Is Who He Is

"My thoughts are not your thoughts,
nor are your ways My ways," says the LORD.

ISAIAH 55:8 NKJV

I've recently read through the *Mark of the Lion* series by Francine Rivers. Escaping to the world of ancient Rome, and following the story of the Jewish slave girl, Hadassah, has been a great treat. Reading Rivers' writing has also fed my Spirit. I once heard her say in an interview that she creates her stories out of deep heart questions she deals with in her own life. After reading her work, it seems clear that Rivers' questions and doubts are ones many others also face. That's probably what makes her books so appealing. Processing those troubling questions through a beautiful piece of fiction is a helpful way for dealing with them ourselves.

My favorite book in the series is *An Echo in the Darkness*.

In it, Marcus Valerian, aristocratic Roman hunk, believes the woman he loves died because of her Christian faith. He goes on a quest through Judea to see if Hadassah's God is real. He meets an old woman named Deborah who tries to guide him. Rebellious and accusing, Marcus asks her at one point, "If Jesus was the Son of God, why did His own people turn Him over to be crucified?"

Deborah's answer is profound. "Because, like you, we expected God to be something other than what He is."

She goes on to explain to Marcus how her people looked for a king who would deliver them from the rule of Rome. They wanted what they wanted, and when God fulfilled His own purpose, instead of theirs, they turned against Him. In anger and disappointment. "Like you," Deborah explains to Marcus. "Yet, it is God's will that prevails."

I love Deborah's explanation (if you can love something God uses to convict you). It made me think of the times I get frustrated with God, disappointed, or downright angry. Each and every time it's because I expect Him to be something other than what He is. I expect Him to behave in a certain way because that's how I would behave. I expect Him to intervene because that's what I want Him to do. I expect Him to provide in the way I see fit. I expect Him to perform up to my expectations. And when He doesn't, I assume there's something wrong or lacking in Him, when the one with the problem is me. In Isaiah 55, God reminds us that His ways are not our ways. We don't think like Him. Our pea brains cannot comprehend all that He deals with on a minute-to-minute basis. He is not going to perform for us just because we ask. He loves us more than that.

Like Marcus Valerian, and God's own people, my sight is limited. I'd settle for what I think is best in a given moment, when what the Lord actually has in mind—His perfect will—is ultimately so much bigger and better.

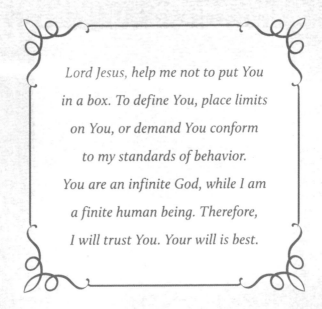

Lord Jesus, help me not to put You in a box. To define You, place limits on You, or demand You conform to my standards of behavior. You are an infinite God, while I am a finite human being. Therefore, I will trust You. Your will is best.

Wherever You Go

Be strong and courageous. Do not be afraid; do not be discouraged,
for the LORD your God will be with you wherever you go.

JOSHUA 1:9 NIV

This past week the nineteen-year-old son of one of my best friends was injured when an Improvised Explosive Device detonated under the vehicle he was driving. He had been in the Army for about a year, and deployed to Afghanistan for only three weeks before the blast. His mother received the call about 7:15 in the morning. It was eight when she called me, crying.

After I got off the phone with her I dropped to my knees beside the couch. I was overwhelmed with sorrow. I had no words to say in prayer, just sobs I know Jesus understood. The day droned on.

I stayed in contact with my friend almost hourly. Finally, that evening she heard from a doctor who explained her son's condition as critical, but stable. He was being transported to a military base in Germany for further evaluation.

By the next day, my friend was struggling with what action to take. She could hop on a plane to Germany, but there was a chance he'd be moved again quickly, to the United States. If she left that day, she might pass him somewhere over the ocean. Panic told her to move. Wisdom told her to be still—to wait.

On the third day, I was praying for her and for her son when I was reminded of Joshua 1:9. The words "with you wherever you go" resonated over and over again in my spirit. I called my friend and we shared the promise of God's Word that tells us Jesus is with us. *Wherever we go.*

I believe that my friend was comforted by those words. As a mother, everything in her flesh cried out to be with her son. And yet, she had to wait for news from the Army. In the spiritual realm, Jesus assured her that He was with her, where she was, and He was also with her son. Jesus was with him in Afghanistan when the blast occurred, with him on the way to Germany in an airplane, with him beside his hospital bed.

The next day brought news he was coming home to the United States. My friend was able to get onto a plane and meet him at the military hospital. It was a bittersweet reunion, full of tears and joy.

Now they are together in an unfamiliar city. He lies in a

room in ICU with a feeding tube and faces multiple surgeries and an uncertain future. My friend sits beside her son's bed and strokes his hand, talks to him, prays over his broken body. Even there, Jesus is. And He will be with them, with us, tomorrow, and tomorrow and tomorrow. With us wherever we go.

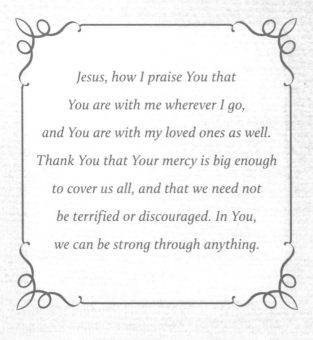

Jesus, how I praise You that
You are with me wherever I go,
and You are with my loved ones as well.
Thank You that Your mercy is big enough
to cover us all, and that we need not
be terrified or discouraged. In You,
we can be strong through anything.

Lessons in Humility

He must increase, but I must decrease.

JOHN 3:30 NKJV

Last summer Harper caught a shark with his fishing pole. More accurately, he caught several sharks. Babies. We held them in our hands. They looked exactly like big sharks, only they were tiny, the size of a small catfish you might catch in the Arkansas River.

I remember one in particular, that Harper took him off the hook, how he stared at me with his strange gold eye. I inspected his little teeth—rows of them, and razor sharp—but too minute to do any damage. His body felt like an earlobe with its total lack of bones. Only its skin was sleek and slick. When I let him go, he swam away in a zigzag pattern with his fin held high out of the water. It was about the size of a tortilla chip, or the sail of a toy boat. But he seemed proud enough of it.

I felt like that proud little shark the other day. I was wearing a blouse that wasn't new, but it might as well have been. I hadn't worn it in years. Since I'd lost a few pounds, I could finally button it. Several people told me how pretty it was. *They're right*, I thought as I washed my hands in the ladies' room sink, *this is a cute blouse*.

As I raised my arm to fluff my hair, something caught my attention out of the corner of my eye. Looking more closely into the mirror, I saw that I had a red drycleaner's tag hanging down from the armpit of my blouse. It had to have been there all day. Through every single one of my Composition lectures.

Things like this happen to me all of the time, so why don't I ever learn? Like that little shark, I can really be thinking I'm the stuff, only to be rudely awakened by the reality that my fin is no bigger than a Dorito.

Another time recently, I was stretching to reach a bargain on the top shelf of Wal-Mart when I noticed a woman staring at me. *She's probably read one of my books,* I thought. As she approached, I imagined she might want to say something about it.

"Are you Gwen Faulkenberry?" She seemed embarrassed, a little shy. I smiled, trying to put her at ease.

"Why, yes, I am." I stepped down from the shelf I had climbed up on and offered her my hand.

She took it, leaning closer to me to whisper. "I hate to have to tell you this, but your seam has split open."

I looked down at my black skirt to find, to my complete and utter horror, that there was a hole at least six inches long, and my white underwear was pouring out of it. What could I do but laugh and thank her? And then slink out of the store as quickly as I could.

God must allow some of these moments to express His own sense of humor. But mainly, I believe He humbles me in order to keep my head out of the clouds and my heart on what really matters. It's not what we look like, or what we accomplish, or what others think of us, or anything else. It's Jesus. Jesus alone.

Jesus, I don't want anything
to keep me from focusing on You today...
who You are, what You've done,
what You are about now in my life
and in the world. Let my mantra be this:
Jesus matters. Jesus alone.

Give Us This Bread

Jesus said…, "The bread of God is the bread that comes down
from heaven and gives life to the world."
"Sir," they said, "always give us this bread."

JOHN 6:32–34 NIV

I love the story in the Bible when Jesus feeds the five thousand with the little boy's lunch of loaves and fishes. Then He withdraws to a mountain to be alone, and the disciples get into a boat and shove off toward Capernaum. When Jesus gets ready, He walks on the water, gets into the boat with his disciples, and goes across the lake. A cool thing happens next: the crowd he had fed the day before tracks him down across the lake and asks Him for more.

Some people interpret this part of the story that the crowd was merely looking for breakfast. That doesn't make much sense to me. Would they really all cross the lake just for the hope of a free fish sandwich? I don't think so. I believe, like us, they were looking for something *more*.

Rather than talking a lot about themselves, they ask Jesus a series of questions. It seems to me that they're trying to figure Him out. He's different. They'd seen, heard, and experienced things with Him the day before that were amazing. They know they want to know Him, they just don't know quite how. They don't yet understand what it all means.

Verses 25–32 contain their questions: When did You get across the lake? What work does God require of us? Will You do another miracle? God gave our forefathers manna. What are You going to do next?

Jesus cuts straight to the heart of what they're seeking. They don't have to say any magic words. He hears. He sees. He knows what they need.

"The bread of God is He who comes down from heaven and gives life to the world."

Oh.

So that's who You are....

That's what this all means.

I love their answer: "Sir, from now on give us this bread."

Can you imagine? They spent the day with Jesus on the hillside. He taught them, healed them, had compassion on them, fed them. The next morning He was gone. But they couldn't let it go—it wasn't enough. They needed more. They had to find Him, whatever it took. So they crossed the lake, searching. When they found Him, I bet they were thrilled! They asked Him question after question, hungry to understand. He was patient as He answered. Then he laid it out for them: *Guys, God has sent me—bread from heaven—to give life to the world.*

"You're the best thing we've ever tasted," they say with tears in their eyes. "From now on, all we need is You!" Yeah, that about sizes it up. All we need is Him.

> *Oh Jesus, You're the best thing*
> *that ever happened to this world.*
> *The One thing that can satisfy*
> *a hungry soul—bread of heaven.*
> *From now on, all I need is You.*
> *No other answers, no other bread.*
> *Just more and more of You.*

Jesus Is Near

For in him we live and move and have our being.

ACTS 17:28 NIV

Mary Beth Chapman, wife of Steven Curtis Chapman, drew from her blog and journals to write *Choosing to See: A Journey of Struggle and Hope*. It's a book about the loss of her daughter, Maria, in a tragic accident. Parts of her story particularly spoke to me, as its theme is believing by faith in order to see Jesus. Her path through suffering has been one of willful choice to believe in the goodness and sovereignty of God, to trust, and to ultimately see His hand at work in the life of her family.

One thing she writes, I believe, can apply to all of us as we seek to live in the presence of Jesus, not only through life's tragedies, but every day: "I need to choose to SEE Christ in every birthday party I drive to, every piano lesson that gets taught, every ballet tutu that gets twirled. God is with me. He isn't waiting until I die for me to be completely healthy. He SEES me now. He is with me now."

My Beloved
You are nearer...
Than the sun that pours through my window at dawn,
Warming me, waking me—inviting me into the new day.
You are nearer...
Than the cool water that I splash on my face
Tingling and sparkling in my skin...refreshing me.
You are nearer...
Than the outside air and the wind that blows
Through my hair—awakening my soul
To the beauty around me and the miracle of life.
You are nearer...
Than the gentle warmth
Of the firelight—softening, illuminating, and soothing
You give me satisfaction and peace
At the end of a day well spent
And, when my head falls softly onto the pillow at night
You are nearer...
Than the moon and stars above me,
Watching over me,
Lighting the world.

Jesus, You are nearer

than my next breath.

You never take Your eyes off me.

Every moment of my day I am

held in Your nail-scarred hands.

Since nothing comes into my life

that doesn't pass through You first,

Help me, Lord, to trust in You.